History

Polity's *Why It Matters* series

In these short and lively books, world-leading thinkers make the case for the importance of their subjects and aim to inspire a new generation of students.

Lynn Hunt, *History*
Tim Ingold, *Anthropology*
Neville Morley, *Classics*

Lynn Hunt

———————

History

Why It Matters

polity

The right of Lynn Hunt to be identified as Author of this Work has been
asserted in accordance with the UK Copyright, Designs and Patents Act 1988.

First published in 2018 by Polity Press
Reprinted 2018 (three times), 2019 (three times), 2021

Polity Press
65 Bridge Street
Cambridge CB2 1UR, UK

Polity Press
101 Station Landing
Suite 300
Medford, MA 02155, USA

ISBN-13: 978-1-5095-2553-9
ISBN-13: 978-1-5095-2554-6 (pb)

A catalogue record for this book is available from the British Library.

Library of Congress Cataloging-in-Publication Data

Names: Hunt, Lynn, 1945-
Title: History : why it matters / Lynn Hunt.
Description: 1 | Cambridge ; Medford, MA : Polity, 2018. | Series: Why it
    matters | Includes bibliographical references and index.
Identifiers: LCCN 2017059695 (print) | LCCN 2017060653 (ebook) | ISBN
    9781509525577 (Epub) | ISBN 9781509525539 (hardback) | ISBN
9781509525546
    (paperback)
Subjects: LCSH: History--Philosophy. | History--Social aspects. |
    History--Political aspects. | Historiography. | BISAC: HISTORY / General.
Classification: LCC D13 (ebook) | LCC D13 .H854 2018 (print) | DDC 901--
dc23 LC record available at https://lccn.loc.gov/2017059695

Typeset in 11 on 15 Sabon by Servis Filmsetting Ltd, Stockport, Cheshire
Printed and bound in the United States by LSC Communications

The publisher has used its best endeavours to ensure that the URLs for external
websites referred to in this book are correct and active at the time of going to
press. However, the publisher has no responsibility for the websites and can
make no guarantee that a site will remain live or that the content is or will
remain appropriate.

Every effort has been made to trace all copyright holders, but if any have been
inadvertently overlooked the publisher will be pleased to include any necessary
credits in any subsequent reprint or edition.

For further information on Polity, visit our website: politybooks.com

Contents

1

Now More Than Ever

Everywhere you turn, history is at issue. Politicians lie about historical facts, groups clash over the fate of historical monuments, officials closely monitor the content of history textbooks, and truth commissions proliferate across the globe. As the rapid growth in history museums shows, we live in a moment obsessed with history, but it is also a time of deep anxiety about historical truth. If it is so easy to lie about history, if people disagree so much about what monuments or history textbooks should convey, and if commissions are needed to dig up the truth about the past, then how can any kind of certainty about history be established? Are heritage sites and historical societies set up to provoke, console, or simply divert? What is the purpose of studying history? This book lays out the questions and offers ways of answering them. It

1

will not resolve all the quandaries, since history is by definition a process of discovery and not a settled dogma. But it can show why history matters now more than ever.

Lying

In one of the highest profile examples of lying about history, real estate developer Donald Trump came to public attention in 2012 by insinuating that then President Barack Obama had not been born in the United States and so had been illegitimately elected president. When Obama presented his birth certificate, confirming that he had been born in the state of Hawaii, Trump immediately retorted that it might be fraudulent, even though he had no evidence that it was falsified.[1] During the presidential campaign in 2016, Trump abruptly changed course and admitted that Obama was born in the United States. He proceeded to take credit for ending a controversy that he helped fabricate. That phony polemic now attracts fewer devotees but other fake ones endure, the most prominent being Holocaust denial.

Politicians and a few writers on the extreme right in Europe have sought their fifteen minutes of fame by denying the reality of the deliberate murder of six million Jews between 1933 and 1945. Denial can take various forms, from asserting that many fewer than six million died or that Hitler and the Nazis had no official plan for genocide to the notion that the gas chambers did not exist. Holocaust denial has become the model for those who want to lie about history; its promoters simply refuse to admit the validity of eyewitness accounts of victims and of those who liberated the concentration camps as well as the subsequent painstaking historical research that has established the names and numbers of those killed and traced the means and motives of the perpetrators in excruciating detail. Although historians can and do disagree about how best to interpret the Holocaust, no serious scholar or reader of history doubts the truth that these murders were deliberate and took place on a mass scale.

Yet despite repeated refutations based on mountains of documentation, and despite the exemplary official and unofficial German efforts to come to terms with those crimes, Holocaust denial still percolates across Europe and the rest of the world, often via social media such as Facebook.[2] It receives robust support at the highest levels of some Middle Eastern governments, which find it useful as part of an anti-Israel policy. On December 14, 2005,

Iranian President Mahmoud Ahmadinejad called the Holocaust "a myth." The official Iranian news agency took those words out of the transcript of his speech as if they had never been uttered, thereby replacing one lie with another.[3] Denials of the Holocaust, however far-fetched or unsubstantiated, have had their effect: an international survey conducted in late 2013 and early 2014 showed that among people living in the Middle East and North Africa, only one-fifth of those who had heard of the Holocaust believed that historical accounts of it were accurate.[4]

Blatant lying about history has become more common owing to the influence of social media. The world-wide web has enabled historical lies to flourish because on the internet virtually anyone can post anything under any name, without prior scrutiny and with no possible sanction. The most outlandish claims circulate widely and gain a measure of credibility just because they are circulating. In this situation, insisting on historical truth has become a necessary act of civic courage.

Historians are rarely subject to the death threats, fatwas, or actual assassinations that threaten journalists, novelists, and opposition figures in too many places, but they have often found themselves at the center of controversy. Authoritarian governments do not like historians known for insisting on inconvenient truths. The popular French historian Jules Michelet was fired from his teaching position by the government of Louis-Napoleon Bonaparte in 1851 because students sometimes left his rousing lectures shouting anti-government slogans. The police had sent undercover agents to attend his classes and then released doctored copies of his lecture notes in the hopes of tainting his reputation. Several of Michelet's colleagues cravenly agreed to censure his teaching to prepare the way for government action. He was then fired from his position at the national archives for refusing to take a loyalty oath after Louis-Napoleon executed a coup against the legislature, which had refused to grant his request for a waiver of his term limit. Michelet, however, was luckier than the hundreds of other opponents of the coup who were arrested and forcibly transported to the penal colony of Cayenne in French Guiana.[5]

As the example of Michelet shows, even normally mild-mannered historians can find themselves in the line of fire in times of political or international crisis. In 1940, *Time* magazine reported that the author of a popular history textbook in the United States, Harold Rugg, had been accused of being a communist who depicted the United States as a land of unequal opportunity and class conflict.

Labeled a "subversive" because he failed to teach "real Americanism," Rugg had his books banned by some school districts and even publicly burned by a school board official in one Ohio town.[6] Textbook authors and in particular textbook publishers will usually go to great lengths to avoid controversy in order to appeal to the broadest possible markets, but as the example of Rugg demonstrates, disputes about historical truth are always lurking around the corner.

Monuments

In mid-August 2017, a public quarrel about the fate of a statue of Confederate General Robert E. Lee ended in violence in Charlottesville, Virginia. White nationalists who opposed the city council's decision to remove the statue from Emancipation Park (formerly Lee Park) paraded with torches on the University of Virginia campus shouting slogans recalling the Nazi era, and the next day their altercations with counter-protesters ended in general brawling near the statue itself. A neo-Nazi drove his car into the counter-protesters, killing one young woman. A monument in place for ninety-three years can provoke strong feelings when it is seen as standing for something repugnant, in this case racism. The Lee statue is not alone. Confederate flags and monuments are in dispute in several states of the former Confederacy: those who want them removed consider them present-day symbols of white supremacy, while those who oppose their ejection cast such efforts as a willful erasure of history. Days after the events in Charlottesville, anti-fascists in Durham, North Carolina, took it upon themselves to topple a statue of a Confederate soldier.

Monuments are not just an issue in the southern United States. Like students at Yale University who wanted to change the name of Calhoun College because it was named after a pro-slavery politician, students at Oxford campaigned for the removal of the statue of Cecil Rhodes because he was a racist and arch-imperialist. These tame versions of proposed monument removal pale next to those that have rocked countless places in turmoil: after the defeat of Hitler, the allies ordered the immediate destruction of all Nazi symbols; after the fall of the Soviet Union, crowds tore down monuments to Lenin and Stalin from Ukraine to Ethiopia; a bronze statue of Saddam Hussein was dismantled in 2003 during the US-led invasion; in 2008 the last statue in Spain of the dictator Franco was removed;

and, to go back more than two centuries, a few days after the promulgation of the Declaration of Independence in 1776, New Yorkers pulled down a gilded equestrian statue of King George III.

Sometimes monument destruction is viewed as vandalism. When the Taliban blew up 1,500-year-old stone statues of the Buddha in Afghanistan in 2001, or when Isis dynamited 2,000-year-old Roman ruins in Palmyra, Syria, in 2015, condemnation of the seemingly senseless demolition of the world's cultural heritage was universal. Islamic militants claimed they were destroying idols, which linked them with a long history of iconoclasm, the breaking or destroying of images, especially religious images, for religious reasons. The term first referred to conflicts in the 700s and 800s over the use of religious images (icons) in the Byzantine Empire. Iconoclasts rejected the growing profusion of images in Christianity and in many instances removed or destroyed them. At the beginning of the Protestant Reformation of the 1500s, especially in Dutch, Swiss, and French cities, mobs sometimes broke into churches and destroyed statues and other decorations considered idolatrous. History therefore seems to provide mixed messages about monument removal.

The ambiguities derive from the nature of monuments. Monuments commemorate: that is, they recall the past and solicit veneration for it. As a consequence, even when they are supposedly secular, such as the statue of General Lee, they inevitably incorporate a kind of religious feeling. Yet monuments are always made for political purposes; they assert power, whether the power of a church, a sect, a political party, or a political cause, such as the Confederacy. Because of this association with power, changes of religious affiliation or political regime often entail monument destruction as well as monument creation. The early Christian churches in Europe were built over the remains of pagan or Roman temples as a way of physically announcing their superiority. In fact, the long history of the destruction of "antiquities" shows that monument destruction is part and parcel of life. (The term "antiquities" only appeared in English in the 1500s, which indicates a new sensibility about annihilating remnants of the far distant past, in this case Roman and Greek remains.)

The paradoxes of monument destruction came most clearly into view in the French Revolution of 1789. The revolutionaries themselves invented the term "vandalism" in 1794 to condemn the overly zealous attempts of some militants to de-Christianize France by seizing gold and silver from the churches, knocking the heads off statues of kings on Notre Dame Cathedral in Paris, and turning churches into temples of Reason. Some churches were sold off and turned into granaries or warehouses. The leaders of the Revolution argued that while symbols of feudalism and monarchy could be legitimately destroyed, those with Latin inscriptions and anything compatible with the spirit of equality ought to be protected. The revolutionaries had already set up the world's first national museum of art in the Louvre palace in 1793 with works confiscated from the crown, the church, and aristocrats who had emigrated. In 1795 the revolutionaries opened the first museum of French monuments with sculpture and tombs scavenged from various religious houses. In short, vandalism and preservation can go hand in hand; the attack on monuments of the past prompted the revolutionaries themselves to think about cultural patrimony. Hated symbols could be preserved if they could be rebranded as art.

The monuments issue can never be definitively resolved. The entire past cannot be preserved because no one wants to live in a museum. Yet some of the past must be preserved in order to maintain a sense of connection and continuity over time. The question is what should be preserved, and that is an inevitably political question. How do we see ourselves, to which past are we most connected, and which parts of that past should be preserved? Every case has to be decided on its own merits, and historical research provides crucial evidence, for example, into the motives of those who commissioned and built the statue of General Lee. Subsequent generations will undoubtedly revisit the decisions. History does not stand still, even if most monuments do.

Textbook Controversies

History textbooks are always being revised, but that only makes them more contentious. One Japanese candidate for governor of Tokyo in 2015 insisted that "As a defeated nation we only teach the history forced on us by the victors." He continued, "To be an independent nation again we must move away from the history imposed on us." Japan was not the aggressor in World War II, he insisted, did not commit the notorious massacre at Nanjing, China, in 1937, and did not force Korean women to serve as "comfort women" (sex slaves) for Japanese soldiers.[7] The controversy was not new. Ten years before, in 2005, Chinese and Korean demonstrators protested revisions in a textbook prepared by

11

the Japanese Society for History Textbook Reform. Claiming that it minimized Japanese culpability for World War II, demonstrators burned Japanese flags and demanded a boycott of Japanese goods.

The Japanese have not been alone in wanting to skew history textbooks toward favorable depictions of their nation. Although a 2011 study of Japanese history textbooks concluded that they largely omitted the country's oppressive colonial regime in Korea (1910–45), the same study also found that Chinese and Korean textbooks focus single-mindedly on Chinese and Korean resistance to Japanese occupation while ignoring the wider context of World War II.[8] Such complaints have a long history. In 1920 a letter to the editor of *The Daily Gleaner* in New Brunswick, Canada, objected that the American-authored world history textbook used in local schools failed to even mention Canada's participation in World War I.[9]

Throughout most of the 1800s and 1900s, and in many cases right up to the present, the effort to instill a feeling of national belonging usually required a positive spin. Textbooks talked about national triumphs or tragedies but rarely about a government's or people's mistakes or misdeeds. The great exception was West Germany after 1945, where from a young age children learned about the crimes committed by the Nazi regime and were constantly reminded of them by visits to concentration camps and to the many memorials and museums found across the country. More common is the recent experience in France, where a law passed in 2005 (later abrogated) insisted that schools teach "the positive role" played by French colonial administrations. A study of French textbooks used since 1998 indeed shows that such books systematically downplay the violence and racism of French colonial administrations in Africa.[10]

Still, this French criticism of textbooks – and the legislative reaction against critical views of French colonial history – makes clear that the traditional feel-good narratives are being questioned and that not everybody likes the questioning. In the United Kingdom, historians now draw attention to the way previous textbooks marginalized the Welsh, Scots, and Irish, treating them as bit players in an overwhelmingly English story. Popular histories of Britain routinely referred to "our Empire" as a way of cementing empire as a part of British identity. Although critics of the empire had repeatedly pointed to its instances of violence and injustice, until a few decades ago British historians continued to focus on the constitutional and reform efforts of the imperial administrations. Historians' recent focus on the downside of empire is only just beginning to influence opinion: a YouGov survey in 2014 found that there were three times as many Britons who felt the empire was something to be proud of compared to those who felt it was something to be ashamed of, and more than three times as many believed that countries colonized by Britain were better off rather than worse off as a result.[11] Opinion would never change, however, if historians did not do the digging into archives that produces new perspectives.

Traumatic events in a nation's life often prompt major revisions of the national narrative, as they did in post-World War II Germany and Japan and in the aftermath of decolonization in France and Britain. As the slow change in assessment in France and Britain shows, however, it can take decades for events to be fully processed. The Civil War and slavery in the United States stand out as prime examples. History textbooks in the pre-Civil War United States did not advocate slavery but they presented a nation in which anti-slavery and pro-slavery forces could co-exist. For decades after the disastrous war, the same kind of accommodationist line persisted as authors blamed the conflict on extremists on both sides. Serious discussion of slavery hardly appeared in US history textbooks before the 1960s, a century after the conflict.

The civil rights movement of the 1960s put the history of slavery in the spotlight, but a sea change in university education after World War II helped pave the way. The proportion of the US population aged 18–24 enrolled in colleges or universities increased from 14 percent in 1947 to 36 percent in 1970 and 54 percent in 1991. The doors opened to social groups long excluded from higher education: young people from the lower classes, women, Jews, African Americans, and other ethnic minorities. The proportion of those enrolled who were female went from 29 percent in 1947 to 51 percent in 1979 and 57 percent in 2014.

Challenges to traditional narratives that focused on the actions of elite white male political leaders might not have been an automatic outcome of these changes, but they were perhaps predictable, given the entry of women, non-whites, and non-Protestants into universities and eventually into university faculties in the United States. The histories of workers, women, African Americans, and immigrants gradually made their way into the textbooks from the 1960s onward, shifting the focus away from heroic figures such as George Washington, Abraham Lincoln, or Theodore Roosevelt toward the previously overlooked contributions of slaves, workers, women, and minorities to the building of a nation. Historians showed, for example, that the supposed "manifest destiny" of Americans to expand westward to the Pacific, a doctrine developed in the 1840s, justified the racial superiority of white Protestant Americans over Mexicans, Native Americans, and Jews and Catholics.

These changes in emphasis and interpretation enraged some people; critics of the critics complained that historians had become obsessed with the politically correct and were failing in their mission to create a positive sense of national belonging. Anger in the United States came to a head in the mid-1990s over two events that critics saw as interrelated. In 1994 the Smithsonian's National Air and Space Museum proposed an exhibition of the plane that had dropped the atomic bomb on Hiroshima and planned to include references to the debate about whether dropping the bomb was morally and politically justified. The same year a federally funded National Center for the Study of History in the Schools proposed national history standards that reflected the new histories of workers, women, slaves, and immigrants that had been gaining steam since the 1960s.

An outpouring of fury greeted both. Senate Majority Leader and future presidential candidate Robert Dole complained that "educators and professors" were engaged in "a shocking campaign

. . . to disparage America." Columnist George Will denounced the "cranky anti-Americanism of the campuses," and Republican Speaker of the House Newt Gingrich maintained that most Americans were "sick and tired of being told by a cultural elite that they ought to be ashamed of their country."[12] The Smithsonian removed almost all of the supposedly objectionable materials, and the national history standards were withdrawn, but historians continued to revise the long-accepted narratives. The politicians won the skirmish, but the historians won the cultural war. No US history textbook can be published today that neglects the history of slavery or discrimination against women and minorities.

Even though a more highly educated population is often more open to discussions of history, textbook controversies cannot be linked in lockstep fashion to enrollment figures. In Russia, for example, the level of university enrollment was already quite high in the 1970s (nearly three times that of the United Kingdom or France in 1971 and about the same as the United States according to Soviet figures), yet textbooks could hardly keep up with the fast-moving events after 1989. In the aftermath of the collapse of the Soviet Union, historians gained greater autonomy, but as Vladimir Putin has consolidated his power, he has also sought to influence textbook writing more directly. Putin's desire to enforce an inspirational patriotic narrative has resounded positively for most Russians.

Still, in Western Europe, especially the United Kingdom and France, discontent with the standard national narratives does seem to follow the trajectory of enrollment figures; in both places enrollment in higher education passed the 50 percent mark in the 1990s, which is when criticism of the national narratives began to bubble up. It is also when gender parity was reached (as many women as men enrolled); in most countries of the world, more women than men are now enrolled in higher education, which represents a staggering change from the 1970s, when only half as many women as men were enrolled. More women does not necessarily mean more criticism, but it does represent a shaking up of the system of higher education. Sadly, it may also explain some of the rising disdain for universities across the Western world; the feminized professions are generally underpaid and less esteemed.

Memory Wars

Textbooks come relatively late in the process of making national memories. The material traces of past events must first be gathered and organized. In recent years, several striking instances of that recollection endeavor have shown how hard it can be to recover the past when forgetting seems desirable, especially the forgetting of events that run counter to a positive national narrative. For more than 150 years, historians debated whether President Thomas Jefferson, the chief author of the Declaration of Independence, had fathered children by one of his female slaves, Sally Hemmings. Until the advent of DNA testing, no definitive answer seemed possible, but when that testing in 1998 made his paternity all but undeniable, a major shift in perspective was inevitable. Well into the 1980s and 1990s, many exhibitions and living museums alike had either obfuscated the role of slavery or made it seem paternal and even benign.[13] In 2012, however, the first major national exhibition to highlight a president's slaveholding activities took place at the Smithsonian's National Museum of American History.

Even more wrenching have been the efforts to recover historical memories in places like Spain that endured not only violent civil wars but also subsequent decades of political repression. Until the military dictator Francisco Franco died in 1975, it was impossible to seriously research the killings that took place during the civil war of 1936–9, much less exhume the bodies of republicans, maligned as "reds," who had been killed without trial and buried in unmarked graves. The empirical work of historical reconstruction began in the 1980s, but not until 2000 was an Association for the Recovery of Historical Memory formed to exhume, identify, and rebury bodies. Attention has turned in recent years to the "lost children," those who died in prison, were sent to state institutions, or had their names changed so that they could be illegally adopted by regime-friendly families.

Memorialization has proved more difficult in Indonesia, where as many as 500,000 communists were killed after an abortive coup in 1965. The general who came to power, Suharto, remained president until 1998, and during that time the killings could not be publicly debated. Textbooks attributed the attempted coup, in which six generals were killed, to the communists and said little about the subsequent torture, beheadings, and mutilations that were carried out by the military and army-affiliated militias who had been whipped up into an anti-communist hysteria. After the fall of Suharto in 1998, the floodgates flew open. Memoirs of imprisoned activists drew public attention, as did previously untranslated works in English. Oral historians began collecting memories of the events.

Reconciliation did not follow, however. In 2000, when a group devoted to exhuming the bodies of the murdered was filming on Java, a Muslim youth group stopped the reburial. The NU (Nahdlatul Ulama, a traditionalist Sunni Muslim organization) burned textbooks deemed pro-communist in 2007 rather than allow a projected textbook reform.[14] In 2013, a museum celebrating Suharto's rule opened in his home town; it was paid for by his brother, who had been convicted of corruption, and its displays justified the crackdown, saying nothing about the innocent people killed.

Countless other examples might be cited of conflicts over memory, but perhaps the most remarkable are the more than thirty truth commissions that have been established around the world since the early 1980s. Many different kinds of societies, from Guatemala to Thailand, have expressed the need for some kind of official mechanism to come to terms with past atrocities committed either during civil wars or under authoritarian governments. A truth commission is a kind of history hearing set up on the premise that the full truth about past murders, imprisonments, tortures, and discrimination must be told if the nation is to move forward. Most truth commissions have been explicitly modeled on the South African Truth and Reconciliation

Commission (TRC) set up by law at the end of 1995 in order to facilitate the transition from the apartheid regime to a democratic one. Because of its influence around the globe, the TRC has been the subject of extensive analysis and debate.

The mandate of the TRC was far-reaching: it included reporting on the nature, extent, and causes of violations of human rights between 1960 and 1994; restoring the dignity of victims by giving them a voice; and even granting amnesty to perpetrators of violence if they divulged all the relevant facts. The task of achieving unity and reconciliation could not have been more daunting. Under apartheid, the white minority (13 percent of the population) controlled almost all the access to land, natural resources, medical care, education, and good jobs. To maintain the white supremacist regime, the authorities had imprisoned as many as 200,000 people, torturing some, forcibly deporting people to unviable "native reserves," and maintaining segregated facilities of all kinds. As resistance to the regime intensified, violence increased on all sides because different political factions within the black communities also fought each other; the regime used violence to put down protests and eliminate resistance leaders, while some in the armed opposition set bombs or killed collaborators, regime personnel, or members of competing oppositional groups.

Despite holding nearly 100 public hearings and receiving more than 21,000 individual testimonies, the TRC itself admitted to the shortcomings of its findings. The white parties supporting apartheid largely refused to cooperate, as did the Inkatha Freedom Party (IFP), the main black opposition to the African National Congress (ANC). The ANC won an outright majority in 1994 in the first parliamentary elections open to all races and set up a government of national unity that included the main white party, the National Party, and the IFP. Nevertheless, the TRC was associated most closely with the ANC, and it was only ANC members who were willing to fully participate. Not surprisingly, then, many whites and IFP members considered the TRC findings biased. Moreover, scholars have criticized the TRC for focusing too much on storytelling and not enough on objective or forensic truth, and studies undertaken on outcomes have shown that at least in the short term, the TRC did not achieve the goal of reconciliation.[15]

These specific complaints should not obscure a larger truth: the recovery of history has become important in virtually every instance of transition from one regime to another. Moreover, this desire to set the record straight is not limited to places transitioning from civil war to peace, from apartheid to black majority rule, or from military authoritarianism to elected civilian government. The history of supposedly stable nations, such as Japan, the United States, or the United Kingdom, is also in question because of elements that have been forgotten, effaced, or repressed and are now coming to the surface. History is always liable to erupt.

Public History and Collective Memory

Even in countries with settled governments, the public appetite for history has never been greater. Memoirs and biographies frequently make the bestseller lists, and some of the most successful films, television series, and video games are set in the past, not just in the United Kingdom and the United States but also in China and many other countries. More than half of the 35,000 museums in the United States are history museums, heritage sites, or historical societies. The National Heritage List for England, first established in 1882, now includes nearly 400,000 monuments, buildings, landscapes, battlefields, and protected shipwrecks. The number of visitors to such sites increased nearly

40 percent between 1989 and 2015. In other words, public interest in history is not simply rising; it's skyrocketing.

Visitors to historical sites do not just want to read labels, look at exhibits, listen to guides, or even watch organized pageants; they sometimes want to enter more directly into the past through historical reenactments and other forms of virtual experience. Living museums such as Colonial Williamsburg in Virginia aim to reconstruct life as it was lived at a moment in the past, in this case the 1760s and 1770s. Tourists stroll streets fronted by eighteenth-century houses and meet people dressed in the costumes of the time who are carrying out the activities that occupied people, women and men, slave and free, in those days. Even more gripping for participants are historical reenactments of battles in which reenactors dress and play the parts themselves. Historical reenactment now influences television and history teaching. In the United Kingdom, United States, Australia, and Germany, history reality programs on TV have featured people living for months in houses exactly as they would have in the past, recording the experiences and conflicts for viewers in the present. History teachers have long used some form of reenactment to intrigue their students, whether putting on period costume for a lecture or having their students take the roles of past historical figures. The advent of digital modeling promises to enhance this trend as ancient Rome, medieval Bergen (Norway), and a neighborhood of eighteenth-century Paris are all now available in 3D, or even 5D in the case of Paris, in which historical sounds and a first-person perspective have been added.[16]

These techniques are reshaping history museums and the presentation of historical sites. Even where digital modeling is not yet in use, material objects are being displayed in ways designed to assure both the authenticity and immediacy of a viewer's experience. Many visitors to the United States Holocaust Memorial Museum report feeling especially moved by the sight and smell of the heap of 4,000 shoes confiscated from Holocaust victims at one concentration camp. Historically minded tourists walk the few preserved trenches of World War I or view the guns, landing ships, and actual planning maps for the D-Day invasion that are now kept in the Utah Beach Landing Museum in Normandy, which is housed in a former German bunker at the landing beach itself. Sometimes the objects come from very long ago. The Jorvik Viking Centre in the United Kingdom takes visitors underground in specially commissioned time capsules to travel back 1,000 years to the Viking era. Animatronic Vikings help bring alive the thousands of pieces of timber, textiles, and other artifacts found in an archaeological dig on the site.

Professional historians have long been critical or even disdainful of historical reenactment and virtual historical experiences because they give priority to the viewer's empathetic identification with people in the past rather than to a deeper understanding of contexts and causes. In other words, walking the preserved World War I trench enables the tourists to feel kinship with the young men who fought there rather than prompting them to ask why the war happened in the first place or why so many young men had to die. Moreover, most virtual experiences must offer an aesthetic appeal in order to attract customers: the slaves at Colonial Williamsburg cannot suffer too much; the Vikings appear mainly at their more peaceful moments; and the trenches are now surrounded by park-like settings.

As multi-media devices and techniques such as virtual reality have become more familiar, it has become impossible to continue to ignore them, and historians have grown increasingly involved with collective memory projects. "Public history" has long engaged many historians, whether working in museums or public and private archives, but until recently, such positions were often considered less desirable than academic posts, and historians in them rarely received training designed for public history. The situation is rapidly changing, as public history becomes ever more important and as a substantial proportion of academic posts have been turned into part-time employment.

Public historians now have their own organizations as well as a recognized place within older associations. A National Council on Public History was established in the United States in 1979, and by 2003 nearly one in five members of the American Historical Association engaged in public history. At least twenty-four US universities now offer a PhD or a PhD-level certification in public history. Nine universities in the United Kingdom offer an MA in public history or a history MA that includes certification in public history; since the first such program only appeared in 2009, growth in this area has been remarkable. An International Federation for Public History formed in 2009 to bring together public historians world-wide; public history is increasingly prominent in Australia, Canada, New Zealand, Brazil, and the Netherlands, and new programs are opening in many other countries.

Collective memories are shaped in many ways, from books and museums to television programs and internet rumors. Whether of traumatic events or national triumphs, collective memories do the most useful and enduring work of shaping identities when they are based on truthful accounts of the past. The public deserves the most accurate possible presentations of historical events and developments, as well as ones that succeed in capturing their attention. The question is how to balance accuracy and artfulness. That brings us to the question of historical truth and how best to ascertain it.

2

Truth in History

Determining historical truth is crucial. Without it, the lies of politicians or Holocaust deniers cannot be countered; monument and textbook controversies will never be resolved; memory wars will continue indefinitely; and the public will have no confidence in the history that is presented to them. Historical truth is two-tiered: facts are at issue in the first tier, interpretations in the second. Although it is possible to separate them for the purposes of discussion, in the actual practice of history they turn out to be interlocking. A fact is inert until it is incorporated into an interpretation that gives it significance, and the power of an interpretation depends on its ability to make sense of the facts.

Facts at first seem to be more straightforward: either Obama was born in the United States or he was not; either six million Jews died in a deliberate effort to exterminate them, or the number is exaggerated or their killing was not intentional. Interpretation, in contrast, is never cut and dried. People can agree on the facts – six million Jews did die in a horrific genocide – and still disagree about how, why, or in what sequence the events happened. Even facts are not as simple as they seem because the past is never settled. New documents, new objects, and new data are always being discovered which can overturn supposedly established facts: DNA testing is invented, for example, and it changes the facts about Jefferson's paternity of slave children. This potential provisionality does not mean, however, that there are "alternative facts," as one Trump administration official notoriously claimed. Those alternative facts were plainly lies: that is, deliberate attempts to mislead the public about the facts. To get at historical truth, then, we begin with facts and how they are determined.

Facts

This is a fact: Barack Obama was born on August 4, 1961, in Honolulu, Hawaii. The truth of the statement is verified by the existence of a document, in this case a birth certificate from the state of Hawaii.

This document is valid because it was issued by a state office with the authority to register births and because no one has produced any evidence that it is false. A series of important points nonetheless emerges from the contrived controversy about Obama's birth. Historical facts rest on documents; documents collected in a systematic manner are more likely to be believed; and facts are necessarily provisional because there is always the possibility that the discovery of evidence in the future might call today's facts into question.

Conspiracy theories arise in the space created by the inherently provisional nature of historical facts. It is possible to imagine, in this case, that Obama's Hawaiian birth certificate was forged on an old typewriter using a blank old form or just produced with some kind of digital technique, but no evidence has been found to support any such conclusion. It is similarly possible to imagine that Donald Trump's birth certificate was forged, or yours, or mine. Obama was fortunate to be born in a state with a department of health and an official registrar. Refugees from war-torn countries flee without clothing, much less birth certificates, and often come from places where government offices have been destroyed in fighting, if they even functioned in the first place. The existence or absence of documents is itself a product of history.

Historical facts are only as good as the documents they rest upon, and some very influential documents in history turned out to be forgeries. One of the most infamous was the "Donation of Constantine," purported to be a decree of the Roman emperor who died in 337 CE. The Donation gave the pope of the Catholic Church authority, both spiritual and secular, over the western part of Christendom; the stakes could not have been higher since popes often fought with kings and emperors for political control. The Donation only began to be cited in the 800s, however, which inevitably raised questions about its validity. In 1440 an Italian scholar, Lorenzo Valla, unmasked it, though scholars still debate the origins of the forgery, which took place most likely in the late 700s or early 800s.

The debunking shows the influence of politics on the search for historical truth. Turned down for a job with the papacy, Valla took a position instead with one of the pope's rivals, the king of Aragon and Sicily, who wanted to wrest control of Naples away from a papal client. Valla's political motivations do not invalidate his demolition. He developed what came to be known as the discipline of philology, that is, the historical study of language, to show that

33

Constantine could not have written the document. The Latin of the document was not Constantine's Latin, he insisted, because it used figures of speech that did not exist in Constantine's time and made references that dated it to a later period. Valla's text did not make much of an impression until a century later, when politics intervened again. Supporters of the Protestant Reformation translated and printed it for a wide audience eager to hear about papal corruption. (The printing press had only just been invented when Valla wrote.) Some still considered the Donation undisputed fact well into the 1600s, though by then the papacy itself no longer did. Fabricated facts sometimes die hard.

Professional historians are not immune to the appeal of clever forgeries. In 1983 several press outlets announced the sensational news of the serial publication of Hitler's hand-written diaries, kept hidden in communist East Germany since the end of World War II. Two leading historians of the Hitler period were asked to examine the volumes and announced they might indeed be genuine, but as publication day approached, they both expressed growing skepticism because there had been no authentication of the handwriting, paper, or ink. Within days of publication, the German Federal Archives announced that their studies of the paper and bindings showed they dated from the post-war period. The hoax had been the work of a former East German living in West Germany who specialized in illegally buying and then selling Nazi memorabilia. Capitalizing on the gullibility of a West German journalist, the counterfeiter had pocketed millions of German marks, and when he was released from prison, he went back to selling forged paintings and drivers' licenses.

As the example of the Hitler diaries shows, to get their facts right historians benefit from a host of scientific techniques that were often developed for other uses. Recent refinements in DNA analysis, for example, make it possible to examine remains from ancient cemeteries in order to determine migration patterns between eastern Europe and Italy in the 500s and thus understand more about the "barbarians" who invaded the Roman Empire. Aerial photography and remote laser sensing first developed for environmental or military purposes have been used to determine the location of Roman roads underneath the current British landscape. Dendrochronology (the study of tree rings) facilitates the dating of Viking ships and the study of climate change in the 1600s. Radiocarbon dating enabled a team of historians and scientists to show that the "Vinland Map," possibly the first map to show the New World, predated Columbus's arrival by almost sixty years. In many of these cases, historians worked directly with scientists to develop their information. Future techniques may challenge some or all of these conclusions; historical facts rest upon the best available evidence. The same is true of scientific facts: Isaac Newton revolutionized the understanding of terrestrial and celestial mechanics, but, like most people of his time, he believed that the earth was only about 6,000 years old. Radiometric dating of meteorites now puts the age of the earth at 4.5 billion years old.

The "best available evidence" sounds straightforward, but it actually depends on what historians or scientists consider reliable sources. Until recently, the best available historical evidence usually meant accounts drawn up by political or religious authorities, such as the Donation of Constantine and the manuscripts or books written by its critics. In other words, the facts are shaped in fundamental fashion by those in charge; they decide what is worth recording. The little that is known of ordinary people's religious beliefs before the age of mass literacy, for example, often comes from priests or police because they could write and had a religious or political interest in recording, but their documents reflect their point of view and their concerns.

The problem is compounded in colonial settings where official documents represent the understanding of administrators or military officers who often had little knowledge of local languages and customs. Catholic officials in newly conquered Mexico treated the beliefs of local Nahuas as the product of Satan's influence and simply persecuted their practices as criminal. To get at the logic of Nahua beliefs, historians had to learn to read against the grain of the Spanish sources and decode the local language, Nahuatl, which employed pictorial writing. In other words, scholars had to look for facts in places previously left unexamined; the best available historical evidence depends in large measure, therefore, on how and why the historian looks for sources. It is rarely a neutral activity.

Despite its occasional reliance on scientific techniques, history is not a science. It is a literary art that uses scientific techniques where relevant but whose fundamental aim is to tell a true story. The truthful part rests on documentation, and in this regard the historian is like a detective, lawyer, or investigative journalist sifting through information, analyzing and comparing sources, written or not, and using every possible forensic procedure to get at the truth, that is, the facts of the case. The story part requires something else: a literary reconstruction that relies on a series of interpretations of the facts. The interpretations make the facts relevant. The world is filled with mountains of historical facts, but we only care about a tiny number of them at any given moment. We care about those facts that enable us to tell the story we want to tell. Telling the story draws our attention to the facts but also frequently stirs up disputes. Historians can tell very different stories about the same event by choosing to emphasize different facts. This cacophony casts doubt on the truth of any one interpretation. If there is so much disagreement about interpretations, how can history make any claim on the truth about the past? Is it just your story vs. mine?

Interpretations

Consider the example of Napoleon Bonaparte, one of the most famous generals and leaders in all of world history. All scholars agree that the Corsican-born general came to power in France in November 1799 and promptly made himself first consul, then consul for life, and then emperor. But they disagree about the interpretations of these facts: Which characteristics of the regime at the time made it possible for a general to take power? What did Bonaparte intend when he came to power? Did he establish a military dictatorship? Why did he fall from power eventually? And even: Was he a good general or not? Did he come to power because the fledgling French republic made bad choices in foreign and domestic policy or because the centuries of long experience with a monarchy conditioned the French to accept a powerful authoritarian leader? Did Napoleon win battles because he was a genius of strategy, a charismatic leader of his men, or just lucky enough to benefit from the clumsiness of his battlefield opponents? The answers depend on how you look at the facts and which facts you choose to emphasize.

The great variability of interpretations casts doubt on the possibility of historical truth. Since historians always write from points of view that are shaped by their personal histories and social contexts, their accounts cannot claim to be entirely objective. When I write on Napoleon, for example, I do so from the perspective of a white, middle-class, woman scholar trained in the United States of the 1960s. I may be less personally involved than a French counterpart, but I still bring my own biases, consciously or not, to the task (as do you as the reader). Although the question of Napoleon's battlefield qualities does not personally agitate me, I am more likely than some to emphasize his efforts to thwart democratic impulses and ensure the subordination of women and children to husbands and fathers. But this positioning does not mean that my account is therefore false, unless I go so far as to argue that these issues are the only ones that matter in considering Napoleon's record. The truest history is often written by people with deep commitments on one side or another of an issue. Blandness is not the same thing as truth.

The greatest historians have been passionate about their quest. The French aristocrat Alexis de Tocqueville wrote what is still the single most influential interpretation of the French Revolution, *The Old Regime and the French Revolution* (1856), because he was horrified by the rise to power in his own time of Napoleon's "lymphatic" nephew, Louis-Napoleon Bonaparte. How could the French repeatedly give up their new-found liberties for a form of democratic despotism? What was the appeal of the Bonapartes? To find answers, Tocqueville went to the official archives of his region and studied in detail the operation of the French monarchy in the 1700s. He became convinced that the monarchy itself had paved the way for the first Bonaparte by destroying the political powers of the nobility and local estates. Tocqueville's passion for the subject propelled him to the archives; his literary skill made his interpretation into a classic that endures.

Tocqueville's claims to historical truth are based on the core standards that are widely accepted among historians: the truthfulness of any interpretation depends on its coherence and its ability to offer an explanation for the important facts. A coherent account is logical; it cites evidence that is germane and does not draw irrational conclusions from that evidence. If I want to argue that Napoleon considered a paternalistic relationship to women and children essential to his brand of authoritarian regime, I will look for evidence in his laws, writings, and even his personal life, but I cannot maintain that the fact that he loved his wife shows he was paternalistic. Such a conclusion does not follow logically. He could have loved his wife and favored any number of different regimes.

More is required than coherence, however. To be as complete an explanation as possible, my emphasis on Napoleon's paternalistic attitude must make sense of as many applicable facts as possible. It does not need to explain his battlefield strategy, but it must account for articles in his law codes concerning women and children, and even perhaps his personal attitudes, though these might have differed from those expressed in official pronouncements. The fact that under Napoleon's law code a wife could not acquire property, contract a debt, work, or make a will without her husband's consent would be a strong piece of evidence for my argument. A critic could still object that Napoleon did not draw up the laws on his own, but though he did not act alone, he did personally supervise many of the sessions that rewrote family law. An interpretation cannot rely only on the facts that fit; it has to stand the test of possible counter-arguments.

Although the close connection between facts and interpretations inevitably raises doubts about historical truth, it also creates constant incentives for more research to resolve those doubts. When my hypothetical critic objects that Napoleon did not write the laws by himself, I am forced to dig deeper and find more evidence of his participation and of his collaborators' understanding of his views. In this way, interpretive disputes produce more facts. Previous interpretations, facts, and debates about them do not disappear from view; they provide the foundation for future work.

Historical Truth and Eurocentrism

These criteria for truth (true facts, coherence, and completeness) appear quite solid, but a bombshell of a problem lurks underneath them. The idea that history writing should aim for truth and a certain measure of objectivity reflects a particular perspective, that of historical writing as it has developed in the West especially in the last two centuries. Although history has always existed as a form of knowledge, university training of historians only took shape in the nineteenth century when it was founded in Germany, France, and Britain. People wrote, read, and studied history for the lessons it could provide for current dilemmas long before the 1800s, and they developed techniques for getting at truth, but universities did not train professional historians. Lorenzo Valla, for example, was a university professor of rhetoric, a field that prepared students to become notaries and court officials. He cultivated an important method of historical research – the philological comparison of texts – but did not do so in order to train scholars in the writing of history.

University training of historians was designed to transmit and improve methods for determining historical truth. One of the founders of history as an academic discipline, the German Leopold von Ranke, famously wrote in 1824 that he did not aim to judge the past in order to instruct future generations; he simply wanted to say "how it really was." Some scholars have criticized Ranke for this supposedly naïve view, arguing that no historian can completely recapture the past; we can only know the past through its remains, the bits and pieces that have come down to us over time. We can never know how it really was. But this criticism is mistaken. Ranke owned up to the partiality of his own view; he admitted that "the intention of a historian depends on his viewpoint." Yet he still hoped to convince readers of history to broaden their perspectives.

At a time when many historians in Protestant countries failed to resist the urge to vaunt Protestant superiority and when historians everywhere in Europe tended to emphasize the distinctness of their own nation's narrative, Ranke was aiming for a more objective view: "strict presentation of facts, no matter how conditional or unattractive they might be," and only then, "development of the unity and progress of the events." Ranke wanted to compel his readers to see the past in a different light. His claim to a more objective view rested on his study of the original sources and footnotes that would enable readers, at least in theory, to verify his rendition.[1]

Ranke's use of a seminar to teach careful comparison and criticism of historical sources to his (all male) students soon had an international following.

Truth in History

The US historian Charles K. Adams wrote in 1889, "At the present day there is no thoroughly good teaching of history anywhere in the world that is not founded on that careful, exact, and minute examination of sources which was originally instituted ... by the German seminar system."[2] Half of the historians who received history professorships in the United States in the 1880s and 1890s had studied in Germany. Ranke was the first foreigner named an honorary member of the American Historical Association after its founding in 1884, and when he died in 1886, Syracuse University in New York bought his personal papers because he had played such a key role in the establishment of the modern discipline of history.

Despite Ranke's own eagerness to range beyond German history, history grew as an academic discipline in tandem with nationalism and a growing conviction of European superiority over the rest of the world. Historians rushed to tell the history of their own nations and focused in particular on the rise of the modern bureaucratic nation state as the preeminent sign of European superiority. European history writing became the gold standard not only for historians in the United States but for those everywhere in the world. South American, African, and Asian students went to Europe to receive doctoral training in history; Western Europe became the model for all historical development; and the historical techniques developed in Europe influenced history writing across the globe. Faced with the challenges of European imperialism, historians in China and Japan, for example, labored to catch up with their Western equivalents.

Given the success of decolonization movements after World War II, it might have been expected that this "Eurocentric" model would have come under fire sooner than the 1990s, but since then, the attacks have come fast and furiously. Dipesh Chakrabarty showed the way with a lament first published in 1992 that has become widely influential:

> That Europe works as a silent referent in historical knowledge becomes obvious in a very ordinary way. There are at least two everyday symptoms of the subalternity of non-Western, third-world histories. Third-world historians feel a need to refer to works in European history; historians of Europe do not feel any need to reciprocate . . . the "greats" and the models of the historian's enterprise are always at least culturally "European." "They" produce their work in relative ignorance of non-Western histories, and this does not seem to affect the quality of their work. This is a gesture, however, that "we" cannot return. We cannot even afford an equality or sym-

metry of ignorance at this level without taking the
risk of appearing "old-fashioned" or "outdated."[3]

Chakrabarty's critique marked a turning point;
though Western models of historical study continue
to exert great influence, from the 1990s onward
historians in Europe and the United States paid
increasing attention to scholarship and scholars
from Asia, Africa, and the Americas. Western universities began to compete for historians from the
non-West. Chakrabarty himself is only one of many
examples; born and educated in India, he did his
doctoral training in Australia and teaches at the
University of Chicago.

Since the standards of historical truth that
developed in Europe accompanied the European
dominance of history writing, complaints about
"Eurocentrism" often include challenges to the
standards of historical truth as well. Combating
Eurocentrism, then, presumably requires attack-
ing that supposedly Western idea of truth. Is the
insistence on primary sources, footnotes, and the
coherence and completeness of interpretations hope-
lessly contaminated by its association with Western
imperialism? In a critique of Chakrabarty for not
going far enough, one literary scholar asserted that
history as a discipline which authorizes knowledge

and truth claims is "deeply accompliced or interwoven with colonialism and cannot be traced back, in any rigorous sense, before the politico-epistemological moment that has taken the name modernity."[4] This assertion simply replaces Eurocentrism with a temporal-centrism in which "modernity" marks the definitive break with all that came before. For historical knowledge and historical truth, such an assertion is untenable; scholars of history claimed authoritative knowledge and truth long before the invention of the university discipline of history.

Neither history nor the concern for historical truth is Western. Chinese scholars have written history since the ninth century BCE and their desire for getting the facts right was so intense that some of them faced execution rather than give in to pressure from rulers to alter them. The twelfth-century Muslim chronicler Ibn al-Qalānisī explained his aims in terms that echo familiarly today:

> I have completed the narrative of events set forth in this chronicle, and I have arranged them in order and taken precautions against error and rashness of judgment and careless slips in the materials, which I have transcribed from trustworthy persons, and have transmitted after exerting myself to make the fullest investigations so as to verify them.[5]

Chinese and Arab Muslim traditions of writing history – and many others as well – thus share the supposedly Western and modern concern with historical truthfulness.

The long history of widely shared aspirations for truth does indicate that history has been and will continue to be written outside the confines of academic history departments; it does not require a university setting in order to aspire to truthfulness. It also shows that the aspiration to truthfulness is not Western. That aspiration predates Western colonialism and imperialism and can be found in many different traditions of writing history. Since the time of the Athenian historian Thucydides, ca. 430–400 BCE, scholars have routinely claimed to be more objective, that is, more truthful, than their predecessors. They could make such claims because they could build on the labors of their predecessors.

It would be a mistake, however, to conclude that history is always the same over time and across cultures. All history, whether written, oral, pictorial, or performative, relies on narrative form, that is, a story that claims to represent the past through some kind of chronological device. Yet these forms come in almost unimaginable varieties; they are so diverse that historians in the West often failed to see that epic poems, pictorial texts and textiles, "talking knots" (the *quipos* of the Incas of South America), and epic narrative singing such as Indonesian gamelan music share a narrative family likeness with the annals, chronicles, and historical manuscripts and books found in the West. They share certain traits, but they also differ in significant ways, and an appreciation for the distinct logics of the different forms expands the conception of history and historical truth. Condescension toward unfamiliar forms of history is falling out of favor now, as is the contempt for more vernacular forms of history generally. The benchmarks of true facts, coherence, and completeness offer a surprisingly wide opening for historical expression.

Even if it is not the only possible form of true historical knowledge, the nineteenth-century European model of historians trained in the university to consult original sources proved to be very powerful. It would not have been emulated in other parts of the world if it had not been able to generate impressive new knowledge of the past. When the University of Tokyo first set up a history faculty in 1887, it only taught European history. Its first professor was a German historian from Berlin, Ludwig Riess, a Ranke student and specialist in English constitutional history. As the history faculty expanded to include Japanese and "Oriental" history, "Western" history consisted of German, English, and French history because they were considered models of historical practice and of the development of the modern nation state. For the same reason, the European history taught in North American universities focused on German, English, and French history until the Cold War of the 1950s prompted greater interest in Russian and Eastern European history.

Similar stories of European influence could be told about many places. The Rankean model made its way to Argentina in the early twentieth century when the University of La Plata asked two professors to survey the historical methods taught in North America and Europe, and especially in Germany. These methods were then implemented for the study of Argentine history and subsequently introduced as well in Mexico, Chile, Peru, Venezuela, and Cuba. Although it is absurd to say, as many have in the past, that South Asians lacked historical consciousness before the arrival of their British colonizers, a leading Indian historian such as Partha Chatterjee can still trace his own interests back to the influence of books written by British historians. In his case, E.H. Carr's *What is History?* (1961) served as "the new testament of the historical method" in the 1960s because it argued for the importance of social and economic history at a time when most historians wrote about political elites and institutions.[6] Carr's lively manifesto had world-wide influence because the debates and controversies that agitated British, French, and German historians continued to shape international historical discussions into the second half of the twentieth century.

As the examples of Chakrabarty and Chatterjee nonetheless suggest, those trained in or inspired by European methods could turn those same methods into tools for challenging Western domination. Like Chakrabarty, Chatterjee resisted the European colonization of everyone else's history:

> History, it would seem, has decreed that we in the postcolonial world shall only be perpetual consumers of modernity. Europe and the Americas, the only true subjects of history, have thought out on our behalf not only the script of colonial enlightenment and exploitation, but also that of our anticolonial resistance and postcolonial misery. Even our imaginations must remain forever colonized.[7]

Needless to say, he had no intention of leaving that colonization unchallenged; he used evidence from original sources to develop his own interpretation of anticolonial nationalism as a form with its own distinctive characteristics that could not be reduced to a pale imitation of Western models.

Although the keen attention to Eurocentrism is relatively recent, historians trained in European methods have been applying those tools for their own purposes since the end of the nineteenth century. At the same time that French, English, and German historians were digging into their government archives to shore up national cohesion in France, Britain, and the relatively new state of Germany (unified only in 1871), Japanese historians used Rankean procedures to support imperial traditions as a way of promoting Japanese nationalism. They even turned the European concept of civilization to their own ends. In 1869, Emperor Meiji ordered a history that would "make clear the distinction between civilization and barbarity," with Japan representing civilization. One of the leading Japanese historians of the first half of the twentieth century, Tsuji Zennosuke, argued in 1950 that Japan had integrated foreign elements such as Confucianism and Buddhism, but had taken them in their original form; as a result, "the essence of Eastern culture is contained in Japan alone."[8]

Argentina presents an even more striking case because so many Argentines had immigrated from Europe. One of the two above-mentioned professors sent from Argentina to study historical methods abroad, Ricardo Rojas, returned and published a report in 1909 titled *The Nationalist Restoration* that made obvious the intended link to Argentine nationalism. In it he argued that to confront the influence of foreign ideas, Argentines needed to develop their own national identity through the teaching of Argentine history in their schools. On the centennial of Argentine independence in 1916 he published *La Argentinidad* (Argentine-ness or the essence of Argentina), in which he extolled Argentina's heroic history and collective memory. He insisted that the independence movement had not been inspired by European ideas but rather had developed out of native sources. In other words, European ways of studying history could be used to buttress non- and anti-European identities.

Provisional Truths

Even when a historical interpretation is based on true facts, is logically coherent, and as complete as a scholar can make it, the truth of that interpretation remains provisional. New facts can be discovered, and the benchmark for completeness shifts over time. Historians have long propped up national cohesion by providing narratives of a nation's supposedly distinctive identity; reading those accounts now reveals an incompleteness unrecognized at the time. This blinkering effect of patriotism is not limited to Europe or the West; it occurs everywhere. Yet before we complacently feel superior to these past efforts, we should recognize that one day our histories will look just as incomplete.

For two centuries, the standard accounts of US history began with a nod to Columbus and then dug in with the establishment of English colonies after the failed first effort at Jamestown in 1607. Although the French and Spanish held much larger tracts of land, historians justified their focus on the English by arguing that the English language and English political and legal institutions shaped the country most profoundly. Native Americans, or Indians as they were called, were largely dismissed. In his popular textbook *An American History*, published in multiple editions between 1911 and 1933, David Savile Muzzey did not hesitate to denigrate the North American tribes, and along with them the contemporary African American population: "They [Indian tribes] had a great variety of games and dances, solemn and gay; and they loved to bask idly in the sun, too, like the Mississippi negro of today."[9] He considered his account coherent and complete without devoting serious attention to Native or African Americans. Muzzey nonetheless found himself accused of writing a "treason text" because he did not write positively enough about the founding fathers of the new republic.

Similar limitations in previous notions of completeness can be found in histories of other settler colonies, such as Australia, but also in those of the imperial nations Britain and France, not to mention India and China. Until recent decades, Australian school texts started with the arrival of James Cook in 1770 and ignored the long history of the Aboriginal peoples. *The Oxford History of Britain*, updated in 2010, still tells the history of "Britain" from the perspective of the English. Wales suffered from misgovernment and disorder; the English brought them peace and a successful government. Histories of France largely passed by slavery or the violence of colonization and told French history from the perspective of the metropole. The lives of slaves or mixed-race people hardly figured at all. Anglophone scholars followed the French lead in this regard. In 1989, Simon Schama's bestselling history of the French Revolution, *Citizens*, devoted one line in a 900-page book to the slave uprising of 1791 in the French colony of Saint-Domingue, and then only to explain discontent in France about the high price of sugar and coffee. French textbooks did not dig into the history of slavery in the French colonies until the beginning of the twenty-first century.

Nationalist historians of India and China had to figure out how to incorporate the experiences of foreign rule that predated imperialist incursions from Europe. In India, two broad narratives still compete for attention. Hindu nationalists have long argued that India is in essence a Hindu nation trying to fight off foreign influences; in these accounts, the Muslim Mughals who ruled over much of present-day India for two centuries appear as foreign, brutal, and violently repressive. Secular nationalist historians argue, in contrast, that religion did not divide Indians until the British took over and fostered communal divisions between Muslims and Hindus; to make their case, they minimize earlier manifestations of communalism. Throughout the twentieth century, Chinese historians emphasized the assimilative power of the Chinese state in order to justify the incorporation of non-Chinese peoples, and some presented the non-Chinese ethnicities as inferior in culture and civilization. The Manchus, who ruled over China for more than two centuries, were described as incompetent, barbaric, and illiterate.

Writing histories that promoted ideas of Western superiority also required a vision that now seems myopic rather than wide-angled. The West was portrayed as the source of technological innovation and cultural advancement ("modernity"); the East was often dismissed with peremptory characterizations, not unlike those used by Muzzey to describe Native Americans. The German philosopher G.W.F. Hegel inaugurated a long history of denigrating the East or Orient in his lectures on the meaning of world history in the 1820s: "The East knew and to the present day knows that only *One* is Free; the Greek and Roman world that *some* are free; the German World knows that *All* are free." The Germans had the benefit of Luther and the Protestant Reformation, which "secured to mankind Spiritual Freedom."[10] To this day many believe that democracy, free markets, human rights, and the rule of law – all variations on Hegel's freedom – are Western values; in this line of thinking it is not clear what values the East might have to offer. For Hegel, the East stood for immaturity, unreflectiveness, subjugation, sensuality, and fanaticism.

As the examples of India and China show, however, the penchant for vaunting one's own ethnic, cultural, or civilizational superiority is not limited to Western countries. In Nigeria, to take a very different example, Yoruba, Igbo, and Hausa-Fulani politicians have used histories of their ethnicities to bolster their competing claims for power within the country. Some historians tried to argue that British colonial authorities effectively created the notion of unified and competing ethnicities, but other historians have contributed to the construction of a sense of ethnicity. There would be no Yoruba "nation" without the pioneering effort of African scholars such as Samuel Johnson to write *The History of the Yorubas* (1921) by recording oral traditions and eyewitness accounts. Under British control, the Nigerians had had to defend themselves against the all-too-common perception in Britain that before the arrival of the Europeans, Africans had no writing and therefore no history. Since independence in 1960, however, Nigerian history has risked division by ethnicity; the Nigerian government's halting efforts to maintain central authority have all too often resulted in dividing resources for historical research by regions identified primarily by ethnic origin. It is very hard to get distance on our own group and see the whole picture.

Do these few examples show that historical truth is impossible? Although they do indicate that absolute truth is impossible, a closer look reveals that the standards of historical truth are incredibly powerful because they facilitate criticism. Have all the relevant facts been considered? Is an explanation, for example, of American identity complete if it ignores the contributions of the French, Spanish, Native Americans, or African Americans? Is a history of Britain entirely coherent if it fails to take account of the Welsh perspective? Historical interpretations are by their nature fragile constructions, always subject to new discoveries and new notions of completeness. The same techniques that were used to reinforce ethnic or national identity and create a sense of European superiority can also be used to challenge the ethnic or national narratives and undermine the Western sense of superiority.

As we will see in the next chapter, those who wish to contest ethnic or national narratives and Western superiority rely on the same standards of historical truth that have been evolving since the early nineteenth century. If there is no agreed standard, then there is no way of determining the truth about the past, however provisional; indeed, there would be no way of even having a debate about that truth. To debate, two or more sides have to agree on the rules for debate, and to win a debate is to make better arguments. If an argument can be improved or disproved, then there is an implicit standard of proof. Discussion and debate are vital because they allow movement in the definition of completeness and encourage those who study history to continue uncovering facts that will change interpretations of the past. They fuel the ongoing democratization of history.

3

History's Politics

Far from democratic at its inception, the academic discipline of history nonetheless opened the way over time to the inclusion of new groups of historians and new kinds of history. What had once been an elite profession, writing about the pasts of elites for the sons of elites, gradually, albeit with considerable foot-dragging, began to admit women, minorities, and immigrants to the profession and to history's pages. The result was a great cacophony of voices raised during fervent debates about history's role in the contemporary nation state and globalizing world. As current monument and textbook controversies show, the disagreements still rage, but the disharmony should not obscure an important truth: debates over history's meanings are vital to the survival of democracy. They are a sign of its health, not its weakness. The opening up of professional history saved it from its own ingrained prejudices.

Elite History

The numbers make clear the elite status of university education in the nineteenth century. In 1870 only 1 percent of US young people aged 18 to 24 enrolled in postsecondary institutions, but this figure is higher than for any other country. In England it was .3 percent and in France .5 percent. The numbers were no higher in Germany or Japan. In this rarefied environment, history did not immediately emerge everywhere as a separate discipline. At the University of Cambridge in England, for example, history only became a subject in its own right in 1873. Before then it was taught as part of moral sciences or law – when it was taught at all.

History in the 1870s meant political history, in particular the history of past elites. Like his counterpart at Oxford, the leading Cambridge historian of the time, John Seeley, believed that history was past politics and politics present history. Elite young men studied history to prepare themselves for politics and government. Indeed, for Seeley, history represented "the school of statesmanship."[1] It did not follow, however, that students studied the history of recent times. At Cambridge, they studied ancient Greece and Rome, medieval Europe, and English constitutional history. The study of ancient Greece and Rome in the original languages had long been considered the cornerstone of any liberal education, and for the new subject of history the classics provided the crucial examples of forms of government and political leadership. Modern Europe had little place, despite Seeley's best efforts; the rest of the world none at all. A professorship of imperial history was established at Cambridge only in 1933. A professorship of US history followed in 1944 in the midst of World War II.

History had an already established place at Harvard College in 1873, but it resembled in most ways history at Cambridge. Every student (they were all men) had to take history in his second year, which consisted of a course on Roman history. History could then be pursued as one of many specializations: all who chose history took Roman and early medieval history in the second year; Europe from the tenth to the sixteenth centuries and medieval institutions in the third year; and in the final year the history of England to 1600, modern history (i.e., history of Europe) 1600–1750, and modern history from the middle of the eighteenth century. These were the required and only available courses of study. Colonial American history only appeared for the first time in 1875, with US history after 1776 following a year later.

History as a discipline was just on the cusp of professionalization in the United States in the 1870s. Medieval history at Harvard was taught by Henry Adams, the grandson and great-grandson of US presidents. He had no training in history, much less medieval history, though after leaving Harvard he wrote a highly regarded history of the United States and the enduringly popular meditation on the French Middle Ages, *Mont St. Michel and Chartres* (1913). In addition to medieval history, Adams taught the first course at Harvard on the history of colonial America. He introduced the seminar method at Harvard, but in his wry autobiography he claimed he did so only because he knew nothing and could "not pretend to teach his scholars what he did not know, but should join them in trying to find the best way to learn it."[2]

When a task force of the American Historical Association offered recommendations for reforming the teaching of history in secondary schools in 1898, it tried to combine the elite focus on ancient, medieval, and English history in the universities with the needs of educating citizens, many of them now from immigrant families. The task force recommended four years of historical study in secondary schools: a first year devoted to ancient history and the early Middle Ages; a second year focused on medieval and modern European history; a third year on English history; and a fourth year, finally, on US history and civics. The rationale given in the report speaks to the concerns of the time: "The student of modern politics cannot afford to be ignorant of the problems, the strivings, the failures of the republics and democracies of the ancient world"; "the character of the forces of modern times cannot be understood by one who examines them without reference to their mediæval origins"; "English history until 1776 is our history"; and when all are taken together, "By a course of this sort, pupils will obtain a conspectus of history which is fairly complete and satisfactory, will follow the forward march of events and will come to see the present as a product of the past."[3] This history would be "fairly complete and satisfactory," in the words of the task force, without any mention of the world outside Western Europe and the United States.

The First Breach

The authors of the 1898 report wanted to develop a history curriculum suitable for both boys and girls, but in so far as history in the university remained "the school of statesmanship," women's places were far from certain. No woman could vote or stand for Parliament in the United Kingdom before 1918, and women only got equal voting rights in 1928. In 1881, Cambridge began to allow women to take examinations but repeatedly refused to actually award women degrees until 1923. Three years later, finally, women got the right to be appointed to university posts. The noted political economist Alfred Marshall was unusual in arguing that women were too inferior mentally to benefit from a Cambridge education, but most university men apparently believed that women should not follow the same educational courses or compete with men for jobs.

Yet because women's colleges had been established at Cambridge in 1869 (Girton) and 1871 (Newnham), some women were able to pursue serious courses of study, attend lectures with male students when the lecturer granted permission, take university-wide examinations, and win scholarships for further study. Eileen Power (1889–1940) was one of the most remarkable of them, becoming a leading medievalist and economic historian. When Cambridge voted once again in 1921 to deny women degrees, she took a post at the London School of

Economics, even though she wrote to a friend, "I do it very reluctantly, because though I have often chafed at being cooped up in Girton, I love the college & I love Cambridge."[4]

Women in the United States got voting rights in 1920, but they enjoyed earlier opportunities for education and professorial posts, in part because of the success of separate women's colleges such as Mount Holyoke (1837), Vassar (1861), Wellesley (1875), Smith (1875), and Bryn Mawr (1885). As public universities were established across the Midwest and West with the aid of federal land grants, pressure grew to admit women to them, too, and by 1900 women already made up more than a third of college students nation-wide. The only female member of the task force that wrote the 1898 report on secondary schools, Lucy Maynard Salmon (1853–1927), earned one of the first undergraduate degrees granted to women by the University of Michigan.

Salmon's career reflected the dilemmas confronting women. She studied at Michigan in the 1870s with Charles K. Adams, an early devotee of the Rankean seminar method. Even though Adams believed women unsuitable for seminar work, he continued to advise her during her graduate studies. She pursued graduate work at Bryn Mawr with future President Woodrow Wilson, then a professor of political science and history. Wilson showed little interest in her studies, but when her MA thesis on the appointing powers of the US presidency was published to acclaim, Vassar offered her a position as its sole instructor of economics, political science, and history. She promptly introduced the seminar method of teaching, and along with her co-authors of the 1898 report she encouraged secondary schools to move away from rote memorization of facts toward critical thinking and the study of primary sources.

The arrow representing the status of women in the history profession did not fly straight up after it took flight. Women's status in the history profession in the United States may have actually declined in the 1950s and 1960s, and many university history departments resisted hiring women into the 1970s. When I was appointed assistant professor of history at the University of California, Berkeley, in 1974, one hundred years after Salmon got her first degree and fifty years after Cambridge consented to grant degrees to women, I was only the fourth woman to be appointed in the department of history. The first, Adrienne Koch, taught at Berkeley between 1961 and 1965; the second, Natalie Zemon Davis, came in 1970. When I was promoted to full professor in 1984, I was the only woman holding such a post

(Davis had left for Princeton) on a history faculty that had forty full professors.

Every female historian of my generation has a similar story to tell: at the beginning of the 1970s, 13 percent of PhDs in history in the United States went to women, but women made up only 1 percent of the history faculties in the major graduate schools. The situation changed dramatically over the next decades: by 2008, women made up more than 40 percent of all new history PhDs and 35 percent of the history faculty of four-year colleges and universities.[5] In 2017, the history department of University of California, Berkeley, listed nine women among its twenty-six full professors. At the University of Sydney in the same year, the history department had fifteen women among its thirty-seven faculty members. In the United Kingdom in 2012, women made up nearly 40 percent of all history academic staff but still only 21 percent of full professors of history.[6] In every country, there are fewer women the higher you go on the academic ladder.

Pushing Open the Doors

The entry of women into the historical profession is only part of the story of opening doors. Minorities, indigenous peoples, and even working-class white students faced obstacles to acceptance that were as great as, and in many cases greater than, those facing women. Few senior scholars expressed their views as forthrightly as the illustrious historian of colonial North America Carl Bridenbaugh. A product of Dartmouth and Harvard who taught at the University of California, Berkeley, between 1950 and 1962, Bridenbaugh could not abide the influx of white male immigrants that took place even before the incursion of women and minorities. In his presidential address to the American Historical Association in 1962 (note: not *1862!*), he lamented the rising number of younger historians of "lower middle-class or foreign origins" whose "emotions not infrequently get in the way of historical reconstructions." Apparently, upper-middle-class (white, male) historians would not suffer from this disability. Perhaps thinking of Jewish men, who had only just then been able to gain a toehold in the profession after decades of exclusion, he concluded that "most of the urban-bred scholars of today" would find it difficult to bring the past to life for students.[7]

Not surprisingly, the obstacles faced by non-whites in the history profession have been especially trying. As late as 1999, non-whites made up only 7 percent of all active history PhDs in the United

States and about 12 percent of new history PhDs. By 2010, the share of racial and ethnic minorities among new history PhDs rose to nearly 19 percent, at a time when, according to the US census for 2010, 28 percent of the population reported as non-white. History in the United States has long trailed other disciplines in this regard. This also seems to be true of the United Kingdom, though it is difficult to find comparable statistics. According to data gathered by the Higher Education Statistics Agency (HESA), in 2015 22 percent of all UK university first-year students, both undergraduate and postgraduate, came from ethnic minorities, which is slightly higher than the proportion of ethnic minorities in the university-age population, but historical and philosophical studies (categorized together) drew only 10.7 percent ethnic minorities among undergraduates in 2015.

Numbers do not begin to tell the whole story, however. In his autobiography published in 2005, John Hope Franklin (1915–2009), the first African American president of the American Historical Association, briefly recounts the racial insults he faced during his life. At age six he was ejected from a train because he inadvertently took a seat reserved for whites; at age 19, he was almost lynched in Mississippi; at age 21, he was refused service while on a date as a Harvard University graduate student; at age 40, he was called a "Harvard nigger" at a local records office in the South (some southern archives simply refused to admit African Americans); and at age 80, he was asked to hang up a white man's coat in a Washington DC club where he was a member, not an employee. The list goes on; it is almost impossible to grasp how difficult it was, and often still is, for minority students to make their way in the university, even when their professors are, as Franklin's were at Harvard, mostly sympathetic.

Recent surveys have shown that ethnic minorities still feel isolated, marginalized, and excluded in UK universities, too. The widely influential Jamaican-born cultural critic Stuart Hall maintained that he did not experience overt racism when he first arrived at Oxford in 1951 on a Rhodes scholarship, though he was "often the only black person in the room." Officially Oxford was polite to black students – "there were so few of us we were regarded as oddities, quaint, rather than embodying any kind of threat." But going into a pub or café, he found "my body was always tensed. . . . I knew the reason people were looking at me was the awkward presence of *difference*."[8] In 2015–16, according to HESA, less than 2 percent of academic staff in UK universities were black, and only 8 percent were Asian.

Since changes in the make-up of students and especially professors of history came slowly at first and only accelerated subsequently, it is perhaps not surprising that what counted as historical study first modified gradually and then underwent more profound transformation in recent decades. As noted above, university studies of history in Europe and the United States first focused on Greek and Roman and medieval European history. National histories took more space at the end of the 1800s, and by the 1910s they had become the dominant offering, at least in the United States. The Harvard catalogue for 1911 lists scores of courses for historical study, and almost all those given for modern European history concern the history of one nation state. England and France got the most detailed treatment, but there were separate offerings on modern Germany, Italy, Russia, and Spain. The era of specialization had dawned. The center of gravity had shifted from the ancient world toward the modern, with the consequence that the nation state would now shape historical study and historical research. Yet US history, though the subject of more courses than in the 1870s, was still overshadowed by medieval and modern European history;

even in the United States, it did not yet occupy the heart of historical studies.

It continues to be a mark of elite status for a US university's history department to give more attention to medieval and modern Europe than to the United States. The 2017 website of the history department of the University of California, Berkeley, listed sixteen professors of medieval and modern European history and thirteen of US history. Yet overall in 2015 more than 41 percent of faculty in four-year colleges and universities in the United States taught US history as compared to 32 percent in European history; the number for European history has been declining steadily since the 1970s, while the percentage of faculty specializing in the non-West has grown. In the United States, then, the decline of Europe and the rise of the non-West have accompanied democratization of the student body, perhaps in part because European history seems not only elite but also white.

Democratization of the subject matter of history followed not so much from the shift in broad geographical areas, however, as from the transformation of approaches. Not surprisingly, new methods got some of their impetus from relative outsiders such as the pioneering women historians Lucy Salmon and Eileen Power. Having begun as a historian of politics, Salmon soon turned her attention to social history, first with a widely reviewed book on domestic service (1897) and then in remarkably prescient essays on the importance of studying what is now called material culture. In "History in a Back Yard" (1911), for example, she used the fence to talk about legal systems of property arrangements and the garden to talk about the global origins of supposedly ordinary plants. Eileen Power made vital contributions to social history (*Medieval People*, 1924), women's history (*Medieval English Nunneries*, 1922), and, like Salmon, also anticipated the current fascination with global interconnections by co-editing a series of travel accounts. She had met her co-editor, E. Denison Ross, during a year's fellowship that took her to India and China on a trip around the world.

Successive waves of new approaches washed over the historical discipline during the twentieth century. They shared an insistence on going beyond traditional political history, that is, the history of kings, parliaments, wars, and treaties. From the first decades of the 1900s, reform-minded historians were calling for new alliances with anthropology, sociology, and economics. The names and dates of rulers and treaties should give way, they argued, to greater attention to the habits of thought and ways of life of ordinary people.

One of the most influential of these approaches came to be called social history because it directed attention to previously overlooked social categories such as workers, slaves, indigenous and colonized peoples, women, and minorities. A few pioneers such as Salmon and Power had pointed the way earlier, but social history finally took off in the 1960s and 1970s as studies of parish registers, census lists, Inquisition records, police documents, conduct manuals, and household account books enabled historians to move beyond parliamentary, diplomatic, and other official sources to get at the lives of ordinary people, whether in times of crisis or over the long haul.

Cultural history followed in the 1980s and 1990s, and, like social historians, cultural historians established their beachhead by criticizing their predecessors. Social historians found traditional political history too narrow to encompass the experiences of ordinary people; cultural historians argued that social history had worked with fixed social categories such as slaves, workers, and women without examining how the categories themselves came to have meaning. Cultural historians studied the categories that people used to understand their worlds. Rather than analyzing the social make-up of crowds rioting during the French Revolution, for example, cultural historians looked at the symbols the rioters challenged and those they favored. Scholars no longer assumed that cultural outlooks would follow automatically from social identities; cultural meanings shaped social identities.

Since the 1990s and especially since the 2000s, historians have been exploring in many different directions at once: global interconnections, the environment, religion, race, and the fate of post-colonial and post-authoritarian societies are all on the agenda. No one approach dominates, and even political history is making a comeback. A recent study of changes between 1975 and 2015 in approaches used by historians in the United States shows that the most favored are women's/gender and cultural history while the greatest declines were registered in social, intellectual, and diplomatic history. Many smaller fields also increased dramatically, but from fairly low levels: environmental, religious, race and ethnicity, and public history. Most striking, however, is the large number of different approaches; women's and gender history was the biggest single category in 2015 but listed by only 10 percent of historians.[9] History now includes just about everything from rubbish in ancient Mesopotamia to surfing in modern-day Sydney. But if it is no longer "the school of statesmanship," then what is it?

History and Citizenship

Although history is no longer "the school of states-manship," it is still "the school of citizenship," as it has been since the advent of mass politics at the end of the nineteenth century. Citizenship, however, is now more capaciously defined. It is no longer just about belonging to your nation, though it is that too, but about how your nation, and therefore each individual in it, fits into a broader global and even cosmic universe. National history will continue to get priority in primary and secondary schools since most acts of citizenship, such as voting, still take place within the frame of nation states. The travails of the European Union have shown that it is not easy to establish multi-national sovereignty in the absence of an underlying multi-national sense of history. For that reason, the European Union has tried to encourage more teaching of European history in its member states. Ironically, European history, and not simply French, German, or British history, has had a much longer history in the United States than in Europe itself because the teaching of history in the United States served first to ... an elite and then, with the coming of World War I and II, to create a sense of common values shared between the United States and its European allies. That role has declined as war in Europe seems unlikely and the US government has become increasingly concerned by developments south of the border and in Asia.

Global history and national history now go together in the United States, not only because the United States' political and economic interests are global but also because immigration has brought peoples from all over the globe to the country. The share of Europeans among the US foreign-born population plummeted from 75 percent in 1960 to 11 percent in 2014 as immigration from Latin America and Asia soared. The national narrative in the United States therefore now includes more about Americans from non-European countries, though Euro-Americans still have pride of place. Even more striking, world history has largely replaced European history as the pendant to US history in secondary schools and even to a great extent in universities. More than two times as many high school students now take the world history advanced placement examination given by the College Board as take the European history one.

Global and national history also go together in the United Kingdom because Britain had a world-wide empire as early as the 1700s and the country draws immigrants from around the world. The foreign-born population in the United Kingdom more than doubled between 1993 and 2015, and by 2015 it constituted 13.5 percent of the population (the comparable figure in the United States was a nearly identical 13.7 percent). The UK government guidelines for the General Certificate of Secondary Education in history (taken by schoolchildren aged 15–16) require at least 40 percent of content to be in British history and mandate attention to three distinct geographical contexts: a locality, Britain, and European or wider world settings. The wider world thus has the same weight as Europe.

The increasing importance of global history can be seen in the make-up of history faculties in the United Kingdom. Among the history professors listed at the University of Cambridge in 2017, less than a quarter focused primarily on Britain, while more than a third focused on Europe and another third on the world outside the West. At the University of Warwick, almost two-thirds of the academic staff indicated some interest in global questions, about half a concern with European history, and about the same an interest in British history. It might be surprising that there seems to be no greater attention to global history in Australia, though by US or UK standards, much of Australian history counts by definition as global history. About one-third of the academic staff in history at the University of Sydney listed their main interest as Australian history in 2017, with slightly more than a third citing European history, 15 percent US history, and 15 percent non-Western history.[10]

The amount of attention given to national history and within national history to different groups will continue to raise questions. In the United States, the Republican National Committee passed a resolution in August 2014 condemning a newly released framework for advanced placement high school courses in US history, claiming that it "reflects a radically revisionist view of American history that emphasizes negative aspects of our nation's history while omitting or minimizing positive aspects." In 2015, a state representative in Oklahoma introduced a bill to require the state's board of education to reject the new framework and teach instead certain "foundational" documents that included Magna Carta, the Ten Commandments, and speeches by Ronald Reagan. The lawmaker was a member of the Black Robe Regiment, which, according to its own website, is a network for teaching "our biblical responsibility to stand up for our Lord and Savior and to protect the freedoms and liberties granted to a moral people in the divinely inspired US Constitution."[11] No separation of church and state for them! The bill was withdrawn after it generated withering criticism, but repeated complaints prompted a revision of the framework to put more emphasis on American exceptionalism and on the founding fathers.

Debate in the United Kingdom has been less venomous, but just as persistent. Concerns about insularity have a long history in Britain. In 1926, school inspectors were already expressing worry that the teaching of history at the primary school level was focused too exclusively on Britain and the British Empire while world history was rarely taught. More attention to world history might prevent the outbreak of further catastrophic world wars, they suggested. Although this hope proved naïve, the weight given to British history in schools periodically produces controversy. When Conservative Secretary of State for Education Michael Gove tried to introduce reforms aimed at bolstering the presence of British history in the school curriculum in 2013, vociferous opposition from teachers and leading academics forced him to backtrack and include more world history and give more leeway for the teaching of immigration and Islamic histories.

Various versions of these disputes are taking place around the world, but they take different forms depending on the local political and geopolitical situation. In Taiwan, scholars and officials argue about the relative weight of Taiwanese as opposed to mainland Chinese history in the school curriculum. In Canada, the argument pits those who want more attention to Anglophone Canadian history against those who want more on Francophone Canadian history. In Brazil, some educators favor more inclusion of the history of indigenous and Afro-Brazilian people. South African teachers have tried to move from a curriculum that supported the racist apartheid regime to one that was more inclusive and democratic.

World history sometimes stands for a greater concern with multi-culturalism, as it does in the United States and the United Kingdom, and in those cases, it represents a conception of citizenship that extends beyond the nation without denying the need for national citizenship. A truly cosmopolitan form of global history is not about to supplant the national history taught in primary and secondary schools, however, and it is not even obvious that such a form would be desirable since history still plays a vital role in creating national cohesion. History has to be written from a point of view, and it is not evident what a cosmopolitan point of view would be: a view from nowhere in particular, from several different places at once, or from outer space?

Still, the global perspective is on the rise, in part because so many different places are now facing the same kinds of contentious issues. New organizations and journals offer a forum for exchanging views about these different national debates across national boundaries. In 2004, the History Educators International Research Network (HEIRNET) took shape and set up a journal, the *International Journal of Historical Learning, Teaching, and Research*, to facilitate such discussion. The *International Review of History Education* serves similar purposes. The 2017 call for papers for a HEIRNET conference references "the current multiple crises of climate change, global conflict, mass migration and rising nationalism."[12] Nationalism has long been history's friend but can on occasion become its chief enemy.

Like textbooks, school guidelines and standards are such a hot-button issue because they go to the heart of national identity, and they are almost always changing because national identity is never fixed once and for all. History makes sure of that. Debates about history take place when a polity is strong enough to allow rethinking and reframing of the nation's past. Shutting down discussion about historical truth goes hand in hand with authoritarianism.

In 2012, fifteen years after the Chinese took over Hong Kong from the British, they introduced a new curriculum that vaunted the communist party as "progressive, selfless, and united," while downplaying the violence of the Cultural Revolution of the late 1960s and early 1970s and the bloody crackdown on dissidents at Tiananmen Square in 1989. Despite protest demonstrations against this brainwashing by tens of thousands of parents, the government enforced the new standards. The authoritarian regimes of Franco in Spain and Antonio Salazar in Portugal had not tried to instill a new ideology such as communism; instead they carefully monitored teachers and textbooks to ensure that they taught the traditional values of obedience to the family, the Catholic Church, and the state. Salazar had himself portrayed in official ceremonies and publications as the natural successor to hundreds of years of Portuguese history. He opposed the democratization of education, arguing that it would undermine the necessary hierarchy of a well-ordered society. Textbooks under the apartheid regime of South Africa, meanwhile, taught that God had ordained an eternal division between white and black.

Although countless other instances might be

cited, the Turkish government's reaction to writings about the mass killings of Armenians in 1915–16 offers an example that continues to trouble international relations. The Turkish government itself admits that hundreds of thousands of Armenians died when the Ottoman Turks deported them from eastern Anatolia. Disagreement concerns the number – 300,000 according to the Turks, 1.5 million according to the Armenians – and especially the intent: Was it a deliberate genocide of a people? The point is not that the Turkish government is wrong in its interpretation that it was not a genocide, since there is room for disagreement, but that it tries to prevent debate; it uses a law against "insulting Turkishness" (changed in 2008 to "insulting the Turkish nation") to threaten writers and scholars who might cast too harsh a light on the events.

Yet for all the efforts of past and present authoritarians to manipulate history and control memory, history and memory have a way of breaking through, thanks in no small measure to the history written and taught by those trained in the discipline. History began as a pursuit by, for, and about elites, but as times changed, so did history writing and teaching. It may not be the first line of defense of democratic societies, but it is actually quite near the front because an understanding of history heightens our ability to pierce through the fogs of willful misinformation that constitute lying. Moreover, history strengthens democratic societies by providing constantly renewable fields for contests over identity. New interests, new researchers, and new sources revitalize those fields. In the process of retrieval, restoration, and debate, a group, a nation, or a world gains a stronger footing. The next chapter explores some of the new methods and approaches that have made history the gateway to comprehending so many different aspects of life today.

4

History's Future

The citizenship taught by history now includes attention to the broadest geographical and deepest temporal reaches. This broadening and deepening reflects changes in the discipline and in the role of history in our lives. New approaches, such as environmental and climate history, have opened exciting new perspectives that respond to concerns facing everyone on the planet. The overwhelming majority of people are officially citizens in a state, but even as citizens in a state or a broader union such as the European Union, each of us has other identities with histories, too. We have the local identities of family, neighborhood, ethnicity, sex, sexuality, region, or anything else that we believe defines who we are. At the same time, we have to confront what it means to be part of a globalizing world facing rapid technological and economic changes, unexpected wars, shocking acts of terrorism, epidemic diseases, massive movements of people, and catastrophic climate events. History therefore has an outsized agenda for the future, yet at the same time, one of its most enduring attractions is the way it can give us perspective on our present-day concerns and even afford a kind of relief from them. That relief is not escapism, however; the distance we can establish from our own preoccupations fosters a more critical attitude toward group or national glorification and an openness to other peoples and cultures. History has its own ethics.

The Globe's History

Each of us lives in overlapping geographical and temporal units that affect our views about history. My taciturn maternal grandfather immigrated to the Midwestern state of Minnesota from western Ukraine; when I was young we called it Russia because Ukraine was part of the Soviet Union. He was a native speaker of German and my grandmother also spoke German as a first language, even though she was born on a farm in western Minnesota. Having been born in Panama had little apparent influence on me because we moved back to Minnesota when I was two years old. Growing up in the 1950s and 1960s, I therefore found myself drawn to the study of European and especially German history rather than Latin American history. I thought I was incredibly lucky to be an American, and I knew I had the advantages that came from being white and middle class, even if my mother had never attended university. At college, I spent many hours discussing with my friends what it must have been like to live in Nazi Germany (my grandfather's name was Adolf!). Would I have resisted or turned a blind eye to what was happening to Jews, communists, homosexuals, Roma, and the disabled?

Every historian has a story to tell about why they chose their field of specialization. I ended up going into French history, ironically, because it wasn't German. Having never visited Europe, but growing up in the same hometown as the novelist F. Scott Fitzgerald, I imagined Paris (correctly) as much more enticing than any German city, especially since the division of Germany into east and west made Berlin off limits for research. French historians in France were developing new methods with worldwide influence, and when I was a first-year PhD student, still in German history, France was experiencing the upheaval of May 1968. So, I decided to concentrate on the French Revolution of 1789, a good revolution, rather than the ascent to power of the Nazis, a bad revolution. Revolution was in the air, and I wanted to figure out what it meant.

We are not restricted, however, to our geographical and temporal circles. If you are attending university or living in a city, you are probably hearing languages from all over the world. You might develop a passion for Indonesian or Nigerian or Peruvian history even with no links to those places, and in the process of studying you would knit new webs of connection. All around you, moreover, whether noticeable or not, is the sedimentation of eons of time, not just the last two or three centuries whose traces are readily visible. History is all about time, and yet, until recently, historians devoted surprisingly little attention to it. That is changing, too.

The discipline of history as it developed in the West has had three major approaches to time: seeking exemplars, projecting progress, and, most recently, what I call, for lack of a better term, "whole earth time." Although it is possible to trace a chronological sequence, all three remain in play.

When history was first taking shape as a university discipline in the nineteenth century, elite young men were fed a diet of Greek and Roman history because the great orators, politicians, and generals of ancient times were considered exemplars, that is, the best possible models of political and military leadership. History can still function in this way because the human imagination can leap across centuries and even millennia to identify with people in the past and learn from their predicaments. Political figures as diverse as former US President Bill Clinton (in office 1992–2000) and former Chinese communist premier Wen Jiabao (in office 2003–13) cite the influence on them of the writings of the Roman emperor Marcus Aurelius (reigned 161–80). "To the wise, life is a problem," the emperor wrote; "to the fool, a solution." Many human issues are perennial.

From the middle of the 1800s to the middle of the 1900s, more or less, the search for exemplars gave way to the second approach to history: the projection of progress. History came to be seen as a single linear progression encompassing every region of the globe. The future came to stand for improvement, rather than degeneration from a previous golden age or simply a product of inevitable cycles of rise and fall. As a consequence, the past could no longer serve as an infallible guide to the present; it had to be overcome, even rejected. Historians now viewed modern peoples as superior to the ancients, and, as a corollary, portrayed Western Europe and eventually the West as superior to the rest of the world. The belief in progress – validated by the triumph of reason and science – helped solidify the Western sense of ascendancy over other regions; the West and its version of secular modernity now represented the future of the entire world.

The German philosopher Hegel laid out an influential version of the progress model, which, for all of its obvious defects, still exercises great intellectual power. In his lectures on the philosophy of history, delivered in the 1820s, he started from the premise that the entire history of the globe was part of one singular history. The Christian God played a part in it, but only through the expression by humans of the divine principle of the spirit of reason. In short, the singular history of the world had to be analyzed in secular terms; religion was subordinated to history and philosophy.

For Hegel, this singular history revealed the progressive triumph of the spirit of reason, but with a distinctive spatial dimension. "The History of the World travels from East to West," he insisted, "for Europe is absolutely the end of History, Asia the beginning." The East represented "the childhood of History."[1] Only Europe, and the especially the German lands, had achieved a mature articulation of reason and freedom. Hegel nonetheless predicted that the United States would move to the center of history in the future. He was not interested in technological or even economic progress; for him the benchmark of progress was the triumph of the bureaucratic state offering life under laws equal for all citizens. He considered slavery inherently unjust, but thought it should only be abolished gradually. Women, however, could never become free individuals in the same way as men; their destiny is defined by the family, according to Hegel, not by an ability to conceptualize freedom in universal rational terms.

Before you start to feel superior to Hegel because you have detected signs of Eurocentrism, sexism, and perhaps racism in his account, you might want to reflect on an irony implicit in your judgment: it is Hegel's sense of how history moves forward that enables you to look "back" at him and see his inadequacies, just as he looked back at Asia or the Greeks and believed he saw theirs. Hegel was convinced that the progression of history revealed the truth hidden in the past and that truth was a kind of inner *telos* (the Greek for "end" or "goal") of freedom. His account was teleological in the sense that everything in history leads to this final end or goal; if world history is the progress in the consciousness of freedom, then everything that happens in history tends toward that goal. Yet we have to admit that it is hard to avoid doing something similar, even if updated for our own times. If history is not a progression toward freedom, then what meaning does it have? Is it about the rise of capitalism, the spread of modernity, the increase in globalization, the growing power of centralizing states – all these or something else? Would a non-teleological history, a history without an inner impulse, even be interesting? This question is still very much up for debate, but at the very least Hegel deserves credit for putting it on the agenda so forcefully.

The belief in progress was not limited to Hegel, historians, or intellectuals in general. Until World War I, despite some siren calls of pessimism, most educated people in the West believed that knowledge was increasing, technology was improving, economies were growing, education was becoming more democratic, and representative government was triumphing. Modernization was occurring everywhere, albeit at different rhythms and with ups and downs. The deadly and seemingly senseless trench warfare of World War I, the economic depression after 1929, and the rise of fascism in the 1930s prompted grave doubts about the narrative of progress. World War II with its horrific number of deaths, the bureaucratically organized genocide of six million Jews, and the invention and utilization of a bomb that could potentially destroy much of life on earth made those doubts about progress even more compelling. Technology could produce death on a mass scale, state authority could serve evil ends, highly educated and prosperous people could support racist policies, and science might contribute to destroying the planet. The belief in progress has not disappeared but it is now in question.

The third approach to time, whole earth time, is just germinating. This term is the best I could devise to bring together various developments in the discipline of history around a deeper and broader sense of time that keeps the earth and its changing environment in focus. This approach argues for a history of the globe in all its dimensions, a conception of history that makes room for every human on earth as well as for life forms outside humans, and a notion of time that recognizes how multiple strands come together to create the temporal environment which we all inhabit but experience diversely. It nonetheless proceeds from one of Hegel's key principles: we all participate in the same history. Unlike Hegel's history, however, a history of the globe for our time does not project Western superiority or the supremacy of any one sex, race, nation, or culture.

A deeper sense of time is essential since the planet itself is now at issue in concerns over global warming and environmental destruction. Over the course of the eighteenth and nineteenth centuries, geologists demonstrated that the earth was much older than the Bible seemed to teach. Until then, most people in the Christian world believed that creation had occurred around 4000 BCE. One particularly influential Protestant cleric, James Ussher, was more specific: in a work published in 1658 he argued that the universe was created, and time therefore began, on the evening that preceded October 23, 4004 BCE. October 23 was the date in the Julian calendar then in use in Britain; it would be September 21 by our calendar. Scientists have continually pushed back the age of the earth from tens of thousands of years old, to millions, and now billions, of years old. The discovery of the greater age of the earth did not immediately change academic historians' conviction about what counted as history; everything before writing was deemed part of pre-history, the subject of archaeology and anthropology, not history. The invention of writing systems dates to about 3100 BCE, not unlike the time frame given by earlier Christian chronologies derived from study of the Bible.

Moreover, the sacred did not disappear with the gradual secularization of historical time in the West. The sense of the sacred was transferred from the Christian God to the ruler by divine right and then to the nation, which itself now became sacred, at least until its sanctity was challenged by the new waves of historical research in the twentieth century. Textbooks, school curricula, and historical monuments have been the subject of such controversy because they touch upon this sacredness. Tearing down a monument or tarnishing a national hero is tantamount to sacrilege in the eyes of some people.

Historians do not often start their histories of the world with the Big Bang, which occurred some fourteen billion years ago, though a few now do, but some attention to the deep history of the earth facilitates a broader view.[2] All of us inhabit a planetary ecosystem as well as more local ecosystems that have taken shape over different spans of time. Recognition of this enables us to see what we share and what we do not share at different scales, from the neighborhood to the planet. Historians are not going to turn into archaeologists or anthropologists, but our view of history is inevitably impacted, for example, by discoveries about early humans and their movement out of Africa long before the invention of writing. Globalization, immigration, and even modernization look different when viewed in the very long-term perspective. We need histories that are deep and wide and histories that are minutely particular and histories of dimensions and units in between because we live in a world of many dimensions, from the local to the national and the global.

History as an academic discipline assumed that humans were the proper subject of history, or at least humans who could write and therefore produce documents. Increasingly, however, historians have recognized that humans do not live and have not lived alone on the planet and do not make history just in relation to each other. People are always interacting with the environment in which they live, with the animals and machines that inhabit the same spaces, and with the microbes and pathogens that make human life possible and sometimes miserable. Awareness of a deeper and broader sense of time has helped draw historians to studying the interactions between humans and their environment, their animals and machines, and their diseases. Humans do not completely control these interactions, as hurricanes, epidemics, recalcitrant animals, and crashing computers all show. The environment, animals, microbes, and perhaps even machines have their own agency in the world; they act independently of humans and shape the human world. Histories of these interactions enable us to recognize that humans are not masters of the universe and that our disregard for the planet and other species has created problems that we must now face.

Research on such questions is now popping up everywhere. Elephants, common in China 4,000 years ago, were steadily pushed southward into smaller and smaller areas as farmers claimed land, destroyed the forest habitat, exterminated elephants who threatened their crops, and finally hunted them for ivory. Medievalists have shown that access to water in Europe shaped settlement patterns and conflicts over property rights. Studies of Native Americans in the United States have demonstrated the devastating agricultural and social effects of the acquisition of horses by some tribes at the end of the seventeenth century. In what has been termed "the Columbian Exchange," the European conquest of the New World opened the way to massive transfers of plants, animals, diseases, and human populations between the New World and Europe. To cite only one more example among many, global cooling in the seventeenth century encouraged Europeans to seek colonial outlets while also hampering early attempts at settlement in North America: extreme weather produced high mortality rates among would-be colonists in Jamestown, for example, and also made the long ocean voyages even more dangerous. Attention to whole earth time is enlarging the canvas of historical analysis, and the pictures that are emerging are often very different from those familiar in the past.

While it might be said that humans, oceans, horses, airplanes, and the syphilis bacterium occupy the same time frame, because humans have invented the time frames that encompass them, they do not experience the progression of time in the same way or even experience the passage of time as progression at all. But more important still, the heterogeneous communities of humans in the present and in the past have experienced and conceptualized time in many different ways. Another of the exciting new perspectives of historical research is the study of different organizations and experiences of time. We live in a globalizing world in which synchronicity and simultaneity are increasingly important, but time zones did not even exist before the end of the 1800s, and they only came into use because of the needs of railroad scheduling. The experiences of nighttime before gas lighting, of seasons before industrialization, and of work before wireless communication are almost as foreign to us now as the notions of time of the pre-Hispanic Maya, for example, who recorded the passage of time in hieroglyphic texts. Like Hegel, the Maya thought of time as revealing an inner truth, but not in a linear sequence. For them time was a circle with endlessly recurring cycles made up of thirteen twenty-year periods; history was therefore also prophecy since the cycles would repeat forever. The past predicted the future.[3] The history of different systems of organizing time shows how contingent and variable those systems have been and so reminds us that ours, too, is a product of history and not universally valid.

The Ethics of Respect

The study of the different ways of organizing time further broadens the perspective gained from histories of the environment, animals, and microbes; these new kinds of history enable us to think about ourselves as a species and not just as members of a family, neighborhood, city, nation, or global region. They also serve as reminders of our limitations; humans do not and cannot live alone on the planet. We might someday imagine living without animals (though I myself cannot imagine life without my dog), but we certainly cannot survive without bacteria, plants, water, or sunlight. The history of humans' relations with their environment, not to mention with each other, points to the need for respect as a necessary element in long-term survival.

An ethics of respect does not translate into easy judgments about matters historical, as we have seen already in the case of Hegel. History involves sets of tensions, between the local and the global, between our own history and someone else's, between academic and popular forms, and even between past and future. The tensions cannot be overcome; they can only be navigated. Local histories, for example, are most convincing when the historian puts a locality in its broader context, whatever that might be. At the other end of the spectrum, global histories, even more than histories of nations, are made up of scores, even millions, of more local units. Nation states have their own institutions that can be studied without necessarily paying much attention to local affairs, but there are few global institutions that provide an adequate framework for a global history. If a scholar wanted to study the global spread of the language of human rights, for example, it would not be enough to study its use in the United Nations or even various non-governmental organizations. The use of the language in many different countries, in governmental and non-governmental arenas, would also have to be included. The global is the local multiplied over and over.

Historians like to burrow in and excavate new channels into the evidence, which means digging along a particular vein or lode, whether it is the biography of a president or prime minister or the routes of the sub-Saharan book trade in Muslim Africa. Tunnel vision is an occupational hazard that is aggravated by the need for specialization in order to make a mark on the field. My doctoral dissertation and first book concerned two towns in France, between 1786 and 1790, and I thought that was immense because it meant comparing two places, albeit in the same country and during a short time span. That choice meant I could delve deeper into the lives of the local people who held office, agitated crowds, and joined the new national guard. I looked at their marriage contracts, their networks of relations, their club memberships, even their addresses. A national history would never have considered those particular people sufficiently important, even though national developments depended ultimately on tens of thousands of such local people. National and global histories are constructed on the building blocks provided by this kind of localized history.

The tension between our own history and someone else's is likewise very productive of new insights. Every nation's or group's history tries to establish its singularity, but identity histories tend to follow similar narrative patterns: the search for roots, the story of overcoming obstacles, and the laying out of challenges still to be faced. Attention to groups that have been excluded in the past from the narrative disrupts the familiar story and leads to the drafting of new narratives. Conflict has been especially intense in settler societies. Should the national history focus on the settlers, or those who were displaced, or both? How should the two or more sides be depicted? The "Aboriginal history wars" of the 2000s in Australia provide a prime example, and they show that resolution, if it comes at all, comes from discussing and debating the tensions, not from trying to make them disappear.[4]

The tension between our history and theirs can extend to a global scale. Earlier writers of the history of the West, as we have seen, have too often presumed the West's superiority over the non-West, but consideration of the long history of Western relations with other regions reveals other possibilities. For the Romans, Europe was the land of the barbarians, the very antithesis of civilization. The thoughts of Greek thinkers such as Aristotle that were eventually posited as the fount of Western civilization came to Europeans via translations from Arabic into Latin between ca. 1150 and 1250. Many historians now agree that the dominant economic power in the world between 1100 and 1800 was China, not Europe. Much of the impetus for Europe's interest in international trade and hence for the development of trans-Atlantic slavery, and even arguably for industrialization, came from the European desire for goods from the east: at first spices, then later, and most significantly, silk, tea, and porcelain from China and calicoes from India. Superiority, whether in trade, technology, military power, or culture, has shifted from region to region around the globe and will continue to shift in the future.

The tension between academic and popular history has taken various forms since the advent of professionalized history in the 1800s. Popular history and historical novels, such as the bestselling ones of Walter Scott, attracted an immense audience for historical writing in the decades after the French Revolution of 1789. Paradoxically, the French revolutionaries' aspiration to break with the feudal past actually encouraged research into the past, which suddenly seemed less familiar and certainly less of a given. But then, as history became a university-based profession, academic historians began to treat popular histories as insufficiently documented, unoriginal, and uninformed by historiographical debates.

At the same time, however, increasing specialization on the model of the sciences rendered academic historical writing ever more arcane and comprehensible only to a small audience of fellow scholars. As specialization increased, the audience for new monographs (even the word sounds boring) shrank. In my field of French history, for example, eleven book reviews and one article were published in English between 1900 and 1910, according to the Web of Science database.[5] Between 2000 and 2010, in contrast, 841 articles and book reviews were published in English on French history. The number of books in the field would bring the total even higher. Who could possibly keep up with the new information and interpretations? Historians narrowed their purview in order to remain up to date.

Still, the distance between academic and popular history is now diminishing, even as both domains are expanding. The American Historical Association's Directory of History Departments and Organizations lists 175 universities offering the PhD in history and more than 12,000 historians. History as a field is very different from the 1880s when Lucy Salmon was named the sole instructor in history, economics, and political science at Vassar College; Vassar today has fourteen faculty just in history. Yet historians now look back to the Salmon days with some nostalgia. She and her colleagues took an active interest in how history was taught in primary and secondary schools, and because their own writings were less specialized, they reached a broader public. Historians are now more aware of what they have lost while gaining academic standing, and more and more of them are trying to write in a way that is more accessible, at the very least to their students. In this case, too, maintaining the tension between academic and popular histories seems the most desirable option; historians have to find their way between the profession's and the university's demands for new information and interpretations, on the one hand, and, on the other hand, the imperative to translate that knowledge into accessible forms.

Balancing past and future, the last of the sets of tensions outlined here, presents unexpected difficulties. We want to know how we came to be where we are now in order to be better prepared for meeting the challenges of the future, but we also want to know where we have been in order to maintain a sense of continuity over time with our families, nations, or the earth itself. Unfortunately, the former – shaping the future – has begun to overshadow the latter – preserving the sense of continuity. But the future is meaningless without the sense of continuity.

As the discipline of history has evolved, and as popular and public history have drawn more interest, the center of gravity of history has shifted toward the present. It is inconceivable to us now that every Harvard University student would have to take a course on Roman history. There is very little agreement among professors or the public about what every educated person ought to know. Even within the discipline of history, which is by definition about the past, research now focuses more often on the last century or two than on the further distant past. Until the 1970s, most scholars who aspired to be considered great historians in Europe or the United States wrote about the foundational periods of state formation, that is, either the Middle Ages or the sixteenth and seventeenth century in Europe or the colonies and the early republic in the United States. In France, the period ranging from the Renaissance of the fifteenth century to the French Revolution is still called "the modern epoch," whereas history after 1789 is "contemporary," by implication more suitable to journalism than history scholarship. Nineteenth-century history got a foothold in France in the 1970s and the twentieth century followed in the 1990s. Now the great historians in France, like those in Britain and the United States, are more likely to be those who write about the twentieth century.

As enrollment figures at just about any institution of higher education will show, students prefer to take history courses on the most recent periods of time. They can still be lured to ancient or medieval history by a charismatic instructor, or a university requirement, but they flock to courses on twentieth-century history. PhD dissertations eventually follow. A recent study of dissertations in history written in the United States in the last 120 years shows that dissertations filed before 1950 were more likely to concern history before 1800 (all fields of history, not just US history). Taken as a whole, however, the overwhelming majority of dissertations focus somewhere in the period 1750–1950.[6] History is in danger, as an academic field, of neglecting much of what has happened in the past.

"Presentism" takes various forms and not just an interest in more recent history. It also includes judging people in the past by present-day norms. Hegel was presentist in the sense that he considered the German conception of freedom as the benchmark for all people, but we are equally presentist when we criticize Hegel for not sharing our understanding of the world today. Presentism is an enduring tension in history's relation to the past; history would have no interest at all if it did not speak to our present-day interests, so we need a dose of presentism, but if we only view the past from our own standpoint, we simply impose our standards on it. The dose of presentism cannot be too high or it will lead us to commit anachronism, that is, the failure to respect chronology. Then the past just becomes an inert mirror of ourselves rather than a place that we can discover and from which we can learn. But the dose of presentism also cannot be too low; sometimes we have to judge the past according to our own values. Would we want to analyze Hitler as just another politician or his treatment of the disabled, Jews, Roma, or Slavs as just another policy option? Getting the right dose of presentism is a constant challenge, and we probably only have a chance of getting it right if our choices are constantly up for discussion and debate.

What do we learn from the past? For me, it is above all else respect for those who came before us. Even with the emergence of a deeper and broader notion of historical time, the two earlier approaches are with us still, and each one provides a unique access to historical knowledge. A globalizing culture still needs exemplars, which can be found in many places and not just ancient Greece and Rome.

The Epic of Gilgamesh, the sayings of the Buddha, the teachings of Confucius, and the oral traditions of countless African or South American tribes are just a few examples. Wisdom is not fundamentally altered by changes in technology, growth in population, or specialization of occupations. Wisdom can be found in learning about how people in the past confronted their challenges.

Progress may be in question, but the very act of telling a story – and all history consists of stories in one form or another – requires a beginning and an end and therefore some sense of progression. Not everything in the past need lead inexorably to the endpoints that we choose for our stories, but the end does influence the way the story is told. The tension between explaining how the end came about and maintaining a sense of the choices being made along the way is one of the most difficult to negotiate when writing history. The story is not exciting if there is no sense of choice, but the story makes no sense if there is no logic to the choices. We still need grand narratives, therefore, though they need not be the story of progress. Thinking about what those narratives should be is one of the undertakings that makes history as a field so exhilarating.

New vistas are constantly emerging. As media have become more omnipresent in our lives, historians have begun to pay more heed to the role of visual representations of all kinds. History as a field has been defined by its relationship to textual documents, and this focus will not disappear, but other ways of delivering information are now being considered, too. In societies without universal literacy, which means all societies before the end of the 1800s, visual forms played a major role: monuments, processions and parades, reliquaries, and woodcuts spoke more directly to ordinary people than did tracts, treatises, or official documents. Similarly, the advent of the digital world is prompting new approaches. Historians now have access to massive databases of all kinds that can be searched in seconds, and the number of them will only increase. Scholars have to learn not only how to use them but also how to evaluate their reliability.

The emergence of new fields such as visual and digital history reminds us that history cannot predict the future but can benefit from the changes it brings. Only our imaginations can predict the future, and we will not know which predictions are right until the future becomes the present. But we can know the past, however incompletely, and we do not need a time machine to get there. All we need is curiosity and a willingness to learn how those before us made sense of their worlds. Why we need to do so was explained by the Roman politician Cicero more than 2,000 years ago. "To be ignorant of what occurred before you were born is to remain always a child. For what is the worth of a human life, unless it is woven into the life of our ancestors by the records of history?"[7]

Notes

Chapter 1 Now More Than Ever

1 Josh Voorhees, "All of Donald Trump's Birther Tweets" (Slate.com, September 16, 2016). Available at http://www.slate.com/blogs/the_slatest/2016/09/16/donald_trump_s_birther_tweets_in_order.html.

2 Carole Cadwalladr, "Antisemite, Holocaust Denier . . . yet David Irving Claims Fresh Support" (*Guardian*, January 15, 2017). Available at https://www.theguardian.com/uk-news/2017/jan/15/david-irving-youtube-inspiring-holocaust-deniers.

3 Karl Vick, "Iran's President Calls Holocaust 'Myth' in Latest Assault on Jews" (*Washington Post*, December 14, 2005). Available at http://www.washingtonpost.com/wp-dyn/content/article/2005/12/14/AR2005121402403.html.

4 Emma Green, "The World is Full of Holocaust Deniers" (*The Atlantic*, May 14, 2014). Available at https://www.theatlantic.com/international/archive/

2014/05/the-world-is-full-of-holocaust-deniers/370
870/.

5 Stephen A. Kippur, *Jules Michelet: A Study of Mind and Sensibility* (Albany, NY: SUNY Press, 1981).

6 *Time*, vol. 36 (September 11, 1940): 62.

7 Rupert Wingfield-Hays, "Japanese Revisionists Deny WW2 Sex Slave Atrocities" (BBC News, August 3, 2015). Available at http://www.bbc.com/news/world-asia-33754932.

8 Gi-Wook Shin and Daniel C. Sneider, eds., *History Textbooks and the Wars in Asia: Divided Memories* (New York: Routledge, 2011).

9 Frances Helyar, "Political Partisanship, Bureaucratic Pragmatism and Acadian Nationalism: New Brunswick, Canada's 1920 History Textbook Controversy," *History Education*, 43:1 (2014): 72–86.

10 Raphaël Granvaud, "Colonisation et décolonisation dans les manuels scolaires de collège en France," *Cahiers d'histoire. Revue d'histoire critique*, 99 (April 1, 2006): 73–81.

11 Will Dahlgreen, "The British Empire is 'Something to be Proud of'" (YouGov.co.UK., July 26, 2014). Available at https://yougov.co.uk/news/2014/07/26/britain-proud-its-empire/.

12 Tom Engelhardt and Edward T. Linenthal, "Introduction: History Under Siege," in Edward T. Linenthal and Tom Engelhardt, eds., *History Wars: The Enola Gay and Other Battles for the American Past* (New York: Henry Holt, 1996), p. 4; Mike Wallace, "Culture War, History Front," in ibid., pp. 185, 187.

13 Warren Leon and Roy Rosenzweig, eds., *History Museums in the United States: A Critical Assessment* (Urbana: University of Illinois Press, 1989).

14 Adrian Vickers, "Where Are the Bodies: The Haunting of Indonesia," *The Public Historian*, 32:1 (2010): 45–58.

15 Audrey R. Chapman and Hugo van der Merwe, eds., *Truth and Reconciliation in South Africa: Did the TRC Deliver?* (Philadelphia: University of Pennsylvania Press, 2008).

16 For a preview of the Rome Reborn project, see https://www.youtube.com/watch?v=28b8FgCUUoQ. For Bergen, see https://www.youtube.com/watch?v=Ue E4LbocQaw. Projet Bretez (eighteenth-century Paris) is available at https://sites.google.com/site/louisbre tez/home.

Chapter 2 Truth in History

1 Leopold von Ranke, *The Theory and Practice of History*, ed. with an introduction by Georg G. Iggers (London: Routledge, 2010), pp. 85–6. On the footnote, see Anthony Grafton, *The Footnote: A Curious History* (Cambridge, MA: Harvard University Press, 1999).

2 Gabriele Lingelbach, "The Historical Discipline in the United States: Following the German Model?" in Eckhardt Fuchs and Benedikt Stuchtey, eds., *Across Cultural Borders: Historiography in Global Perspective* (Lanham, MD: Rowman & Littlefield), p. 194.

3 Dipesh Chakrabarty, *Provincializing Europe: Post-colonial Thought and Historical Difference* (Princeton, NJ: Princeton University Press, 2000), p. 28.

4 Qadri Ismail, "(Not) at Home in (Hindu) India: Shahid Amin, Dipesh Chakrabarty, and the Critique of History," *Cultural Critique*, 68: 1 (2008): 210–47, quote p. 214.

5 Chase F. Robinson, *Islamic Historiography* (Cambridge: Cambridge University Press, 2003), p. 143.

6 Partha Chatterjee, "Introduction: History and the Present, " in Partha Chatterjee and Anjan Ghosh, eds., *History and the Present* (London: Anthem Press, 2006), p. 1.

7 Partha Chatterjee, *Empire and Nation: Selected Essays* (New York: Columbia University Press, 2010), p. 26 (essay first published in 1991).

8 John S. Brownlee, *Japanese Historians and the National Myths, 1600–1945: The Age of the Gods and Emperor Jinmu* (Vancouver: UBC Press, 1997), pp. 82, 157.

9 David Saville Muzzey, *An American History* (Boston: Ginn, 1920), p. 20.

10 Georg Wilhelm Friedrich Hegel, *The Philosophy of History*, trans. J. Sibree (New York: Colonial Press, 1900), pp. 104 and 441.

Chapter 3 History's Politics

1 George Kitson Clark, "A Hundred Years of the Teaching of History at Cambridge, 1873–1973,"

The Historical Journal, 16:3 (1973): 535–53, quote p. 540.

2 Henry Adams, *The Education of Henry Adams: An Autobiography* (Boston: Houghton Mifflin Company, 1918), p. 302.

3 American Historical Association, "The Study of History in Schools (1898): A Report to the American Historical Association by the Committee of Seven, 1898." Available at https://www.historians.org/ab out-aha-and-membership/aha-history-and-archives/ archives/the-study-of-history-in-schools.

4 Maxine Berg, *A Woman in History: Eileen Power, 1889–1940* (Cambridge: Cambridge University Press, 1996), p. 108.

5 Robert B. Townsend, "What the Data Reveals about Women Historians" (American Historical Association, May 2010). Available at https://www. historians.org/publications-and-directories/perspec tives-on-history/may-2010/what-the-data-reveals-ab out-women-historians.

6 Royal Historical Society, "Gender Equality and Historians in UK Higher Education" (January 2015). Available at https://royalhistsoc.org/wp-content/ uploads/2015/02/RHSGenderEqualityReport-Jan-15.pdf.

7 Carl Bridenbaugh, "The Great Mutation," *The American Historical Review*, 68: 2 (1963), 315–31, quotes pp. 322–3, 328.

8 Stuart Hall (with Bill Schwarz), *Familiar Stranger: A Life Between Two Islands* (Durham, NC: Duke University Press, 2017), pp. 157–8.

9 Robert B. Townsend, "The Rise and Decline of History Specializations over the Past 40 Years" (American Historical Association, December 2015). Available at https://www.historians.org/publica tions-and-directories/perspectives-on-history/decem ber-2015/the-rise-and-decline-of-history-specializati ons-over-the-past-40-years.

10 In every case, I consulted the websites of the universities. For the University of Cambridge, I counted the main concern of those listed as professor of history. For the University of Warwick, I used their online system of finding expertise, which allows staff to list more than one interest. For the University of Sydney, I counted all academic staff.

11 On the advanced placement standards controversy see, for example, Lauren Gambino, "Oklahoma Educators Fear High School History Bill Will Have 'Devastating' Impact" (*Guardian*, February 20, 2015). Available at https://www.theguardian.com/ us-news/2015/feb/20/oklahoma-ap-history-bill-dev astating-dan-fisher. On the Black Robe, see http:// www.blackrobereg.org/.

12 https://www.dcu.ie/stem_education_innovation_glo bal_studies/events/2017/May/HEIRNET-2017-Con ference.shtml.

Chapter 4 History's Future

1 Hegel, *The Philosophy of History*, pp. 103 and 105.

2 The most influential of the efforts to recast history much further back in time can be found in David

Christian, *Maps of Time: An Introduction to Big History* (Berkeley: University of California Press, 2011).

3 Nancy M. Farriss, "Remembering the Future, Anticipating the Past: History, Time, and Cosmology among the Maya of Yucatan," *Comparative Studies in Society and History,* 29:3 (July 1987): 566–93.

4 Bain Attwood, *Telling the Truth About Aboriginal History* (Crows Nest, New South Wales: Allen & Unwin, 2005).

5 https://webofknowledge.com.

6 Ben Schmidt, "What Years Do Historians Write About?" (Sapping Attention, May 9, 2013). Available at http://sappingattention.blogspot.com/2013/05/wh at-years-do-historians-write-about.html.

7 Peter G. Bietenholz, *Historia and Fabula: Myths and Legends in Historical Thought from Antiquity to the Modern Age* (Leiden: Brill, 1994), p. 57.

Further Reading

History has become increasing self-aware as a discipline in recent years, and readers will find no shortage of guides to what it is, what it has been, and what it might become. Despite the proliferation of such works, many history faculties no longer require any study of the philosophy or history of history as a discipline. Historians tend to just go on with their own researches and therefore pay most attention to the debates within their own subfields, which are still defined for the most part geographically and temporally: for example, ancient Greece, late imperial China, Civil War and Reconstruction in the United States, or twentieth-century Mexico. The study of the history of history, sometimes called historiography, is made all the more difficult by the recent emphasis on global history and the need to take into account traditions of history writing that are very different from those in the West. All but the last of the general books listed here focus on Western history writing.

Further Reading

E.H. Carr, *What is History?*, with a new introduction by Richard J. Evans (Houndmills: Palgrave, 2001).

Although already forty years old in 2001 when it was republished with a new introduction, Carr's little book is still one of the liveliest and most provocative introductions to historical study. It is especially noteworthy for its discussion of causes, progress, and the slippery nature of facts, but best of all it is a delight to read.

Ludmila Jordanova, *History in Practice*, 2nd edn (London: Bloomsbury Academic, 2006).

First published at a time when public history was just making a mark, this concise volume by one of Britain's most wide-ranging historians offers a very accessible introduction to the study and writing of history. It is especially strong on locating history in relation to other humanities and social science disciplines and on the crucial but often neglected topic of periodization.

John Tosh, *The Pursuit of History: Aims, Methods and New Directions in the Study of History*, 6th edn (London: Routledge, 2015).

The subtitle says it all; this book aspires to cover just about everything that concerns the contemporary study of history. Lucid and thorough, it reviews all the recent developments in history in considerable depth.

It also offers helpful sidebars on leading historians, past and present, and on key concepts and terms.

Sarah Maza, *Thinking about History* (Chicago: University of Chicago Press, 2017).

Carr provides a great introduction but this book brings him up to date. The author succeeds admirably in explaining the stakes of current controversies about history and the wide range of new approaches, from the history of science to the history of things. It also gives a very good sense of specific authors and their books.

Georg G. Iggers, Q. Edward Wang, and Supriya Mukherjee, *A Global History of Modern Historio-graphy*, 2nd edn (London: Routledge, 2016).

It may not be perfect because it tries to do so much, but this book is an essential first step toward integrating the various historiographical traditions around the world. It may be more useful as a kind of reference work for the purposes of comparing ways of approaching history, but it could also spark new ideas about the writing of history.

The above list of introductory works could be much longer, but other books merit consideration because they take up specific momentous issues that have had great resonance among historians. Here are some of the works that have created enduring intellectual excitement.

Further Reading

Joyce Appleby, Lynn Hunt, and Margaret Jacob, *Telling the Truth about History* (New York: W.W. Norton, 1994).

Although now more than two decades old, the book is included here because its explanations of the stakes in arguments about historical truth have yet to be replaced by something better. Our book took a middle-ground position, against any notion of absolute truth in history and against the denial of any truth at all in history. In short, we argued for provisional truths, a position, as might be expected, much like the one taken in this book but developed with more attention to the philosophical issues.

Dipesh Chakrabarty, *Provincializing Europe: Postcolonial Thought and Historical Difference* (Princeton, NJ: Princeton University Press, 2000).

The author has led the way in dethroning Eurocentrism in historical studies. He has not been alone in doing this, but his book has been especially influential, perhaps because he himself is so well versed in Eurocentric history. He has now moved on to a concern with climate change, which may signal an important shift in the way we approach history more generally. Only time will tell.

Joan Wallach Scott, *Gender and the Politics of History* (New York: Columbia University Press, 1988).

If one book could be credited with establishing gender history as a field, this would be it. Scott has been the subject of frequent criticism because she enthusiastically embraced what is called the "postmodernism" of the French thinkers Michel Foucault and Jacques Derrida, but she has shown how the skillful use of such theories can transform a once stodgy discipline such as history.

Stuart Hall, *Cultural Studies 1983: A Theoretical History*, edited by Jennifer Daryl Slack and Lawrence Grossberg (Durham, NC: Duke University Press, 2016).

Hall effectively invented what is now called "cultural studies" by bringing together sympathetic critiques of Marxism and French structuralism and adding to them a dose of postmodernism and an interest in race, which until then had been absent from virtually all forms of French theory and Marxism, too. These lectures from the 1980s are an excellent introduction to the kinds of theoretical debates that agitated literary scholars and historians in the 1980s and 1990s and still do now.

No invitation to further reading would be complete without some consideration of the most exciting ventures into new domains.

Further Reading

Iain McCalman and Paul A. Pickering, eds., *Historical Reenactment: From Realism to the Affective Turn* (Houndmills: Palgrave Macmillan, 2010).

Long disdained, historical reenactment poses fascinating questions about the forms of history created for, and in this case by, the public.

Mark Elvin, *The Retreat of the Elephants: An Environmental History of China* (New Haven, CT: Yale University Press, 2004).

Although this remarkable study places too much emphasis on the "war" between humans and elephants, the author does try to understand developments from the point of view of the elephants.

Daniel Lord Smail, *On Deep History and the Brain* (Berkeley: University of California Press, 2008).

Smail is a true adventurer in all things historical. In this book he insists that historians should no longer limit themselves to a time frame delimited by writing or to their conventional sources and methods; he argues for a neurohistory that brings brain–body chemistry into historical analysis.

Peter N. Miller, *History and Its Objects: Antiquarianism and Material Culture since 1500* (Ithaca, NY: Cornell University Press, 2017).

Further Reading

Concerned with things and time, this book is written in a very personal voice, unlike most historical studies. It is therefore a very good place to pursue further some of the themes raised all too briefly in these pages.

Index

Index

Index

Index

Index

Index

135

Index

Index

Index

Index

Index

Index

Index